Carving Birds In Wood

By E. J. Tangerman

Sterling Publishing Co. Inc. New York
Distributed in the U.K. by Blandford Press

Picture Credits

This book is made possible by the cooperation of publishers who have granted permission for me to include selected illustrations from my earlier books. These include:

Whittling and Woodcarving (1936—Dover Publications, Inc., New York): Figs. 1, 15–17, 24, 25, 28, 29, 145, 146, 153, 154, 181, 196, 197, 338.

Design and Figure Carving (1939—Dover Publications, Inc., New York): Fig. 94.

The Modern Book of Whittling & Woodcarving (1973—McGraw Hill Book Company, New York): Figs. 26, 27, 75, 76, 89, 90, 92, 98, 110, 111, 114, 118, 126, 127, 137, 138, 140, 189, 190, 191, 203, 208, 225, 233, 267, 269, 274, 280, Page 4 photo.

1001 Designs for Whittling & Woodcarving (1976—McGraw Hill Book Company, New York): Figs. 3, 4, 8–10, 23, 30, 31, 37, 41–44, 52–55, 82, 86, 88, 91, 113, 116, 119, 124, 125, 142, 175, 179, 195, 198, 199, 204, 205, 207, 209, 211, 212, 219, 220, 228, 229, 235, 236, 239, 241, 242, 258–263, 281, 293–295, 297, 300–303.

Carving Wooden Animals (1981—Sterling Publishing Co., Inc., New York): Figs. 71, 80, 132, 134, 158, 167, 168, 176, 177, 231, 251, 279.

Relief Woodcarving (1981—Sterling Publishing Co., Inc., New York): Figs. 240, 266, 268.

Carving the Unusual (1982—Sterling Publishing Co., Inc., New York): Figs. 56, 99, 100, 117, 130, 133, 144, 155, 156, 174, 202, 257, 271, 277.

Basic Whittling and Woodcarving (1983—Sterling Publishing Co., Inc., New York): Figs. 2, 7, 81, 103, 108, 142, 143, 147, 148, 150, 224, 226, 227, 270, 289, 291, 292.

Library of Congress Cataloging in Publication Data

Tangerman, E. J. (Elmer John), 1907–
Carving birds in wood.

Includes index.
1. Wood-carving—Technique.   2. Birds in art.
I. Title.
NK9704.T247 1984   731.4′62   83-24227
ISBN 0-8069-7866-X

Contents

The stylized eagle above is Swiss. It is not feathered, but gouge-scalloped; vees indicate feather tips. Oldest American carving extant is the wooden eagle at left, found near Lake Okeechobee, Florida. Indians shaped it with fire, then gouges of shark teeth. Sketch by Kent Bailey, courtesy of National Carvers Museum Foundation.

Enter the World of Birds

BIRDS HAVE ALWAYS FASCINATED MAN because they do quite easily something that man can only envy—they can fly. Primitive man gave them special reverence and supernatural power. Our own Indians revered the eagle, the owl and the raven; some used them as totems. The Indians learned to make crude decoys to attract live birds within arrow range. White pioneers learned from the Indians, even elaborated their imitations.

We are still making decoys, but the modern ones are often too elaborate and expensive to be wasted in hunting birds. They are designed to attract buyers who collect decoys. Also, the United States has become a nation of bird-watchers; they too are attracted to bird models.

As a result, more birds are carved in the United States than any other country in the world, either in toto or per capita. However, almost all of the birds carved are realistic birds; somewhere along the line in the United States has been lost the old-fashioned custom of carving stylized or caricatured birds, of making birds as toys, of incorporating them in designs.

This is not true among people of Java, Bali, Japan, Yugoslavia, China, and even Denmark and Sweden. They produce beautiful stylized birds in exotic woods, with or without tinting, and many are really original works of art. Some of their carvers are expert in combining birds in a design.

Africans and Dayaks still worship the hornbill. Papua New Guinea has the fish eagle in its coat of arms. Guatemala has the quetzal. Germany had the eagle, Russia the double-eagle. Napoleon used the eagle as an imperial symbol. And don't forget that the sophisticated United States still uses the eagle in its coat of arms and on its money!

This book is my effort to bring together all these diverse ideas about birds and to show how they are carved for whatever purpose. Many are drawn from my earlier books, but some are new. I have tried to explain the basics of carving realistic model birds, but in many instances this becomes a really specialized craft that is more painting than carving, and many books devote themselves totally to it.

My emphasis here is on other ideas and techniques, on birds for design and decoration and on ways to broaden your carving range. Designs are graded for difficulty, insofar as that makes sense, first in-the-round, then in relief. Included are tips on woods and tools, warnings on pitfalls, suggestions on finishing, and patterns. Happy carving, and may all your birds sing!

E.J. Tangerman

CHAPTER I

Woods and Tools to Use

Some pointers and suggestions to save time, money and trouble

MANY OF THE BIRDS CARVED in the United States in recent years are as accurate copies of the living birds as the carver can make them, so they are often more of an exercise in painting than in carving. If the bird is to be painted anyway, it may as well be carved from a soft, easily workable wood like white pine, basswood, aspen or the jelutong recently imported from Indonesia. Also, it can be assembled from blanks of convenient size and shape, one the body, another the neck and head, for example, when glass eyes and metal cast or formed legs are added. Blanks can be sawed out with a coping saw or band saw, and either whittled, if small, or power-sanded or rasped to general shape if larger.

The decoy, a very popular current carving because of the ease with which it can be made and sold, can range from simple blocks glued at the neck to bodies assembled from pieces to reduce core weight so they will

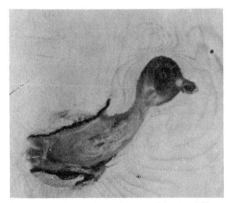

Fig. 1. Believe it or knot, this duckling required no carving. It is a knot in a ponderosa pine board, sawed and planed over 50 years ago.

Fig. 2. Stylized nighthawk carved from spalted (partially dry-rotted) curly broadleaf maple. It is 2½ × 4 × 9 in (6.4 × 10.2 × 22.9 cm). Grain suggests feathers.

6

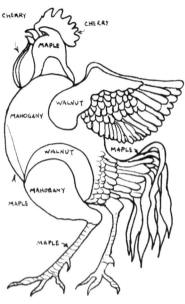

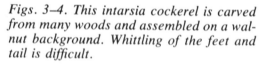
COCK – an assembly

Figs. 3–4. This intarsia cockerel is carved from many woods and assembled on a walnut background. Whittling of the feet and tail is difficult.

float at a realistic level. It can also have individual or feather groups glued in place to give an effect of verisimilitude—even of wind ruffling feathers!

If birds are to be finished without tinting or painting, a harder, better-looking wood can be used, even one with some visible grain or figure. Many native woods are employed for such carvings, and much more depends upon the carving, so both knives and chisels may be used; some pros even have special tools or punches to make eye and bill details. Many carvers use pyrographic needles to burn in the veining of feathers (which tints the veins simultaneously).

There are, as a matter of interest, several schools of thought on feathering. One group holds that the body should be monolithic: Any feather details should be carved from the solid. Another sees nothing inconsistent in carving and veining individual feathers or small groups and gluing them in place to get greater realism. A third group, the natural-wood advocates, among which I am included, uses a wide variety of woods, depending upon the effect desired.

Sometimes the grain or shape of the natural wood controls the shape of the piece, as well as its finishing. Thus, carvers in the southern Appalachians may use buckeye, walnut, cherry, maple, pear, apple, holly, mimosa, or even the recent import, paulownia. Western carvers may use red alder, cedar, redwood, broadleaf maple or other local woods. Any carver may use twisted or diseased or partially dry-rotted (called spalted or doty) wood to create a unique, stylized bird, and any may use mahogany, ebony, or some other imported wood because of its color and finish. I have recently, for example, combined teak and rosewood, with inserts of holly, beefwood and purpleheart, to make some Korean wedding ducks.

In panel or relief carving, the range of woods is also very wide unless the panel is to be painted. Also, it is quite common to carve thin, flat silhouettes of birds in flight, for wall or plaque mounting or to be combined in mobiles. Typical examples of these will be shown, and the woods they are made from described. For such carving, it is almost mandatory to have a set of carving tools; the knife is a bit clumsy for carving concavities, reverse curves, and long outlines, such as those for wing shapes or feathers. For larger birds, like life-size eagles, a chain saw is a decided help in roughing, as it is in making the birds on totem poles or the like.

I know of one North Carolina pro, Sue McClure, who uses a double-bitted axe, sharp as a razor, for roughing out blanks, which included a mother hen with a group of chicks clustered about her. Mrs. McClure in 1975 had an order for 35 life-size turkeys for an executive who gave them as Christmas presents to employees—so there was a deadline. The double-bitted axe made it possible for her to deliver—even though the birds were basswood assemblies, stained. (The proceeds enabled her to relax by buying a new car for her own Christmas present.)

Select a wood that meets your immediate need, soft if you're going to paint anyway, harder and of a suitable color if you plan a clear finish, straight-grained unless you have figure or grain in mind. Holly is our whitest wood, and is matched by English sycamore. Maple is off-white and quite hard. Cedar, depending on variety, can be quite pinkish-brown and odorous. It also may tend to split easily, something that is quite important in panel carving or if you plan outstretched wings.

Cherry is hard and gives a good finish and an agreeable pinkish-brown tone. Walnut is harder and tends to be very dark when finished. Mahogany is softer and varies in color and density, depending upon the source ("mahogany" has become a word used for a variety of woods, including lauan, primavera or limba [white mahogany] and others). Some mahogany is coarse, open-grained and tends to split, but most finish well.

ONA KILLS ÑANDU
(Indian strangles ostrich)
Argentina-mahog.
(Villalba)

Figs. 5–6. Ona kills Ñandu, an 11½-in (29.2-cm) Argentine sculpture in mahogany by the master, Villalba. "Ona" is a Tierra del Fuego Indian, "ñandu" a kind of ostrich. The Indian entangled the bird's legs with his boladeros to catch it. Texturing of skirt, feathers and hair is random.

Apple is hard and light-colored, pear hard, possibly with twisting grain, and a bit darker. Among the exotic woods, I find teak completely tractable and best for polyglot panels of birds and the like—it resists weather, warping and insects best, but is expensive nowadays. Woods like purpleheart, greenheart, beefwood, amboina, and the others of African and South American origin tend to be difficult to carve. Of them, rosewood is probably most interesting and can be gotten in a range of colors from reddish to almost black, some even including greens and yellows. Local woods like alder, mesquite and ironwood give quite interesting results and good natural finishes.

Ken Thompson, a woodcarving friend from Brighton, Colorado, says: "The choice of wood is easy, Tange: cedar for the cedar waxwing, black ash for blackbirds, redwood for cardinals, pussy willow for catbirds, blue spruce for bluebirds, sage for sage hens, canary wood for canaries, and maybe horse chestnut for sparrows and mesquite for the Texas state bird, the mosquito." To which I might add: purpleheart for the purple martin, scarlet haw for the scarlet tanager, beefwood for the cowbird, sapwood for the sapsucker and growth wood for the peewee.

Finish, by the way, on harder woods should not be shiny; it should have a soft glow. This can be obtained by waxing or polishing with Kiwi® natural shoe polish (as they do on macassar ebony in Bali). A somewhat higher sheen can be obtained on coarser-grained woods with a coat or two of shellac, rubbed down with steel wool, preceding the waxing. Generally speaking, I prefer *not* to sand a natural-finish piece but to leave tool marks that prove the piece is hand-carved; sharp tools will leave almost polished cuts on most hard woods.

A well-made jackknife with two or three blades is the most versatile knife to use—it can be used anywhere. Get one with carbon-steel blades; they hold an edge better than stainless blades, although they do tend to rust from pocket sweat unless kept well-oiled. Blades should be short, under 1½ in (3.8 cm) long normally. One should have a pen or spear point; another should have a B-clip or a more rounded point (see Fig. 11). For home use, a fixed-blade knife may be better and safer. I prefer one with a curved cutting edge, but many carvers use knives with a straight edge and curved back. The curved tip gives me greater clearance when I'm cutting in close spots with the knife end—which I do a lot.

There are also handles available that will take interchangeable and disposable blades. They offer greater variety in shape of blade and a more

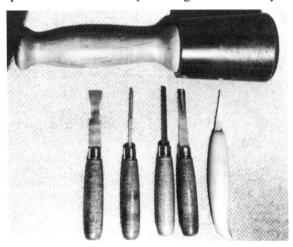

Fig. 7. A selection of small chisels and a plastic-coated lightweight mallet are a good combination for beginning relief carving of birds. Here are ½- and ¼-in (12.7- and 6.4-mm) firmers, two gouges of different sweep, and my favorite knife—a special. Not shown, but useful, is a V-tool.

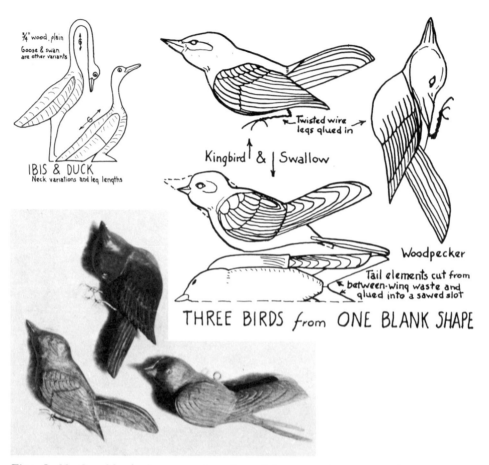

Figs. 8–10. One blank shape can be adapted for several varieties of birds. In the example above and at upper right, three different birds come from the same blank shape. At upper left is an example of Israeli design for production carving—a constant body shape for four species. Variations in neck and leg length produce ibis, duck, goose, or swan, with grain direction changed to suit.

comfortable handle, but the chuck may tend to unscrew, particularly if you carve left-handed. You should be able to carve, at least to some degree, with either hand; it makes for convenience and allows you to use the paring cut, the most easily controlled cut, more often. Also, blades on some types of chuck knives are too thin and weak, and interchanging can be a nuisance—although I know some carvers who can't sharpen blades well, so they discard them as they do razor blades.

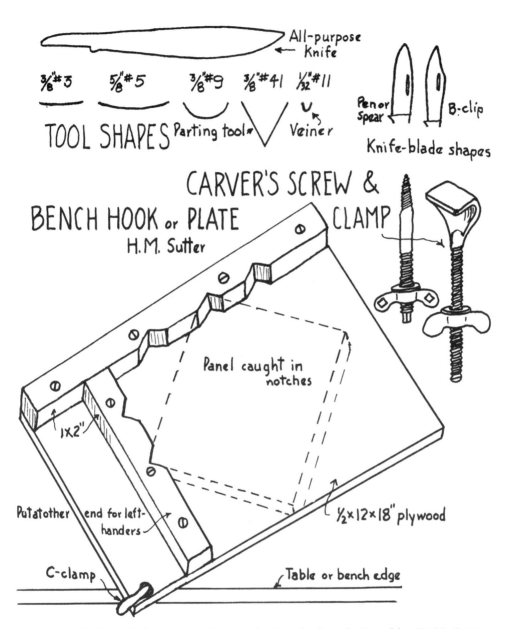

All-purpose Knife

3/8"#3   5/8"#5   3/8"#9   3/8"#41   1/32"#11

Pen or Spear   B-clip

TOOL SHAPES Parting tool V Veiner

Knife-blade shapes

CARVER'S SCREW &
BENCH HOOK or PLATE CLAMP
H. M. Sutter

Panel caught in notches

1x2"

Put at other end for left-handers

1/2 x 12 x 18" plywood

C-clamp

Table or bench edge

Fig. 11. Basic tool shapes and sizes and a bench plate designed by H. M. Sutter. The bench plate will hold a panel for relief carving, yet allow ready movement. The knife blades are my preferred shapes. Carvers' screws are traditional for holding blocks for sculpture.

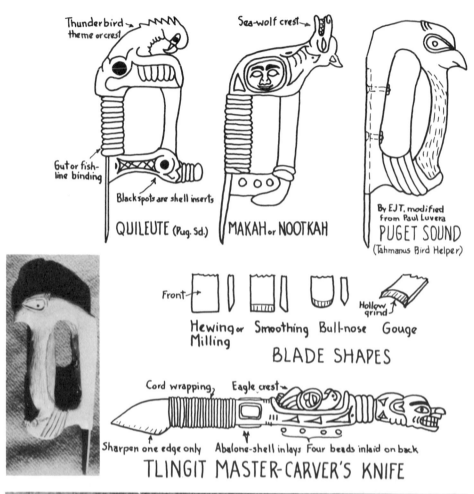

Thunderbird theme or crest

Gut or fish-line binding

Black spots are shell inserts

QUILEUTE (Pug. Sd.)

Sea-wolf crest

MAKAH or NOOTKAH

By EJT, modified from Paul Luvera

PUGET SOUND
(Tahmanus Bird Helper)

Front

Hollow grind

Hewing or Milling   Smoothing   Bull-nose   Gouge

BLADE SHAPES

Cord wrapping   Eagle crest

Sharpen one edge only   Abalone-shell inlays   Four beads inlaid on back

TLINGIT MASTER-CARVER'S KNIFE

Figs. 12–14. Bird motifs were common in carvings of the Northwest Coast Indians. I made these copies of their designs. The D-adze is a reground file with maple handle (see Fig. 245). The carver's knife is mahogany binding a piece of reground power-hacksaw blade. Inserts are abalone shell and red-top pins.

13

As far as chisels are concerned, I suggest small and inexpensive ones for the carver of life-size birds. Conventional woodcarving chisels are longer and require two hands for carving, particularly if a mallet is used. I find that even the small chisels can be used quite successfully with a plastic-coated mallet. Suggestions for the use of chisels are given in Chapter XIII.

Don't start out with an elaborate set of many expensive tools; buy a few varied shapes of gouge, a V-tool and a small firmer (flat chisel, sharpened from both sides). Supplement them with other tools as you find the need. This goes for either in-the-round or relief carving; unless you do very high relief, which requires undercutting behind elements, many special chisel shapes are almost useless.

I have sketched the shapes and sizes of a beginner set suggested by H. M. Sutter, who has taught relief carving for years, as well as his design of a bench hook or plate for holding small panels at convenient angles. Decoy carvers tend to use universal vises with a screw top to hold decoy bodies. It is cheaper to use a carver's screw, set through a hole in the bench into the block. Small sizes can be held in the hand—the best vise of any, but also the most vulnerable to the tool that slips. Watch out!

In bird carving, it is faster and easier to saw out a blank with a coping saw, or whack out a bigger one with a chain saw or band saw. You may also like to use rasps or drawknives for shaping larger bodies, then finish with chisels or the knife.

Figs. 15–17. These are early tries of mine at the whittling trick of wetting a soft-wood blank, then splitting a section into thin blades which can be spread into a fan. Blades are held by interlocking tip notches or by threading, as in the peacock (Fig. 17, far right). Fig. 15 (left) shows a simple bird and fish. Fig. 16 puts a fan-winged and -tailed bird in a cage, with its ancestor, the double ball-in-a-cage.

CHAPTER II

Fan Tails and Wings

An old whittling trick goes very modern and dramatic

AMONG THE FIRST WHITTLING TRICKS I learned was the fan—produced by splitting blades along the grain of a prewhittled shape from a thoroughly soaked piece of pine or basswood. Later, I evolved the flying bird and flying fish, which were simply fans added to a formed body—or rather, cut from it. I thought these were breakthroughs, until I discovered that my idea had been anticipated by a hundred years or so in Scandinavia.

The technique, however, whether or not it is a hackneyed whittling trick, is worthy of review in discussing whittled birds. It is not complex, requiring only a compatible wood, thoroughly soaked, a sharp knife and steady hand. I have shown here my early experiments with fish and bird, plus a more elaborate bird-in-a-cage, a logical and obvious combination with the traditional ball-in-a-cage. It has been made in pine. The bird has been carved in line with the grain of the major piece, with blocks left for splitting or shaving into the wings and tail. The wings must obviously be

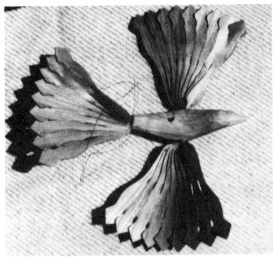

Fig. 18. A Swedish fan-winged and -tailed bird. This 6-in (15.2-cm) one has separately made wing units set into drilled holes.

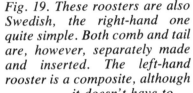

Fig. 19. These roosters are also Swedish, the right-hand one quite simple. Both comb and tail are, however, separately made and inserted. The left-hand rooster is a composite, although it doesn't have to be. Comb and wattles are set in slots; wings and tail are glued in place. Note the shavings within shavings to create wing and tail curls.

cut quite short, or else spread out to clear the body so it can be right-angled into the proper position in the cage.

Swedish carvers make a finer bird, with thinner wing pinions (undoubtedly the result both of repetitive manufacture and sharp knives), but also on occasion utilizing separately made fins set into holes in the bird body. This violates the old whittling rule of having a monolithic piece—but the Swedish pieces are made to sell! They also violate another rule: Some are stained a brilliant blue, which is scarcely the color of any wood I know.

The Swedish work, however, has been eclipsed by modern Japanese carving. The wood is still a very soft and straight-grained white pine, and

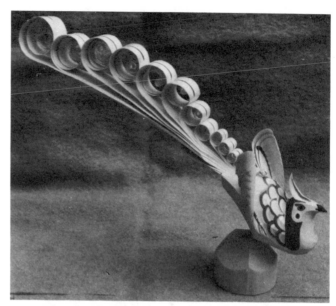

Fig. 20. Monolithic except for the base, this Japanese bird of paradise has wide but short curls for the wings and long, individually curved curls for the tail. Over-all length of this bird is 12 in (30.5 cm); painting enhances the body shape. The crest is also a shaving combination. Grain direction is vital.

Fig. 21. Wings of the hawk in this pair are broad, thin shavings from the rear sides of the base, while the tail is longer shavings peeled up from below. Note the block shape of the body and the feet painted on a cutaway step. The peacock is a graduated fan, cut progressively from the bottom in lengthening, then shortening, blades.

Note: Added fillips are a ruff above the peacock's tail fan, and another below it, short curls in each case. The base is later cut at an angle; the cutoff piece is reversed and glued in place as a support stem, in turn glued to a larger base. Both carvings have details added in oil colors.

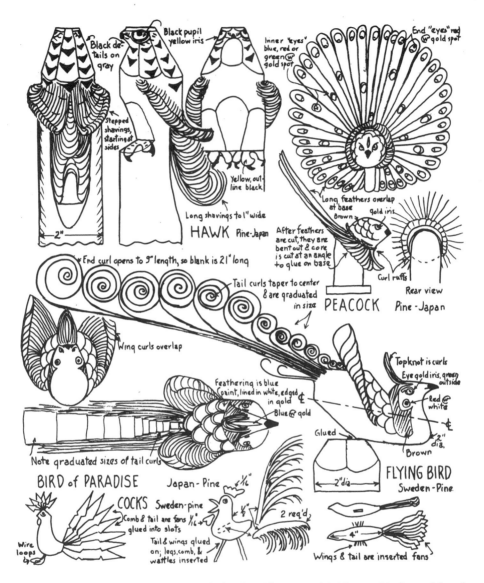

Black details on gray

Black pupil yellow iris

Inner "eyes" blue, red or green w/ gold spot

End "eyes" red w/ gold spot

Stepped shavings, starting at sides

Yellow, outline black

Long shavings to 1" wide

HAWK Pine-Japan

Long feathers overlap at base

gold iris

Brown

After feathers are cut, they are bent out & core is cut at an angle to glue on base

Curl ruffs

Rear view Pine-Japan

PEACOCK

* End curl opens to 9" length, so blank is 21" long

Tail curls taper to center & are graduated in size

Wing curls overlap

Topknot is curls

Eye gold iris, green outside

Red w/ white

Feathering is blue paint, lined in white, edged in gold

Blue w/ gold

Glued

2" dia.

Brown

Note graduated sizes of tail curls

BIRD of PARADISE   Japan-Pine

2" dia.

FLYING BIRD Sweden-Pine

COCKS Sweden-pine

Comb & tail are fans glued into slots

Tail & wings glued on; legs, comb, & wattles inserted

Wire loops

2 req'd

Wings & tail are inserted fans

4"

Fig. 22. The Japanese have carried the fan idea to a highly sophisticated level, producing elaborate effects by varying curl thickness and location. These sketches give some idea of design complexity as compared with the simpler Swedish ones below.

18

Fig. 23. Another tricky Japanese idea is demonstrated by this figure of a cock in the lobby of the old Hotel Fujiya in Miyanoshita. A life-size carving of a cock body is mounted on a support post at the desk, with its long, elaborate tail carved on the post and painted white to match the bird. Thus it contrasts sharply with the stain finish of post and desk and the red tori, or gate, miniature.

the knives are still very sharp. But the Japanese attain effects I couldn't have dreamed. They make closely spaced wing elements on a hawk, curled slightly, and widely spaced elements on another bird's tail, sliced so thin they curl upon themselves. They make long individual blades into a peacock tail by distorting the cut blades into a continuous circle while they're wet, so they'll stay in position when they dry. They also arrive at the body shape of the bird with a very few strong cuts; in the case of the hawk, they really plane, rather than shape. They also use judicious spots of color to enhance the effect of the otherwise almost dead-white wood.

CHAPTER III

Basics of Model Birds

Principles, silhouettes and patterns for familiar species

As a Boy Scout studying birds, I carved them in-the-round, usually life-size, with primitive feathering denoted by paint. I worked from bird guides that were rather primitive, too, supplemented by observation of the bird being carved, so poses and coloring were not too bad. The local scout executive, a non-carver, became interested and soon was turning out birds that rivalled mine; he added such ideas as inserted bills and tails, feet made of wound wire, and bodies rasped to shape. That was in the early twenties, when model birds were made by bird-watchers and decoys were whacked out by hunters or woodworking shops without too much regard for shape or color—ducks are not as discriminating as collectors.

When I wrote an article on how to carve birds for a now-defunct magazine called *Science Illustrated* in the middle forties, most of the questions I got were from ornithologists wanting to know how to get proper color and texture on the birds they made for exhibit; the birds made for exhibit lasted longer than stuffed ones. (The emphasis already was on painting, not carving.) Bird watching became more common thereafter, and such organizations as the Audubon Society and swank sports stores like the late

Fig. 24. Life-size birds carved by I. K. Scott, Boy Scout executive, in 1922.

Abercrombie & Fitch in New York began to sell model birds and bird "scenes" at modest prices.

Then the collecting generation came along—and the rest is history. In increasing numbers, plumbers, engineers and lawyers deserted their professions to carve birds for sale, particularly duck decoys. Shows were established, annual competitions held, book after book written. Certain names began to emerge and decoys were taken down from barn lofts, dusted off and sold for increasingly high prices. Craft stores and mail-order houses offered glass eyes and cast legs.

As usual with Americans, new techniques were developed, such as veining feather surfaces with a pyrographic needle, carving feathers individually or in small groups and gluing them in place, as well as the discovery of irridescent and special-effect paints. Also, as usual with Americans, various schools of thought developed; some carvers felt the bird should be monolithic (except maybe for a separately carved and glued-on head), others felt separate feathers were the best answer. There were similar schools in painting techniques. There still are, because the market continues to proliferate. And there were—and are—a few bird sculptors who disdain the glass eyes, metal legs and artificial bases and make carved birds without delineating feathers at all.

In the face of such expertise, real or assumed, it is presumptuous of me to do any more here than outline the simpler methods for carving familiar birds. I have not gone in for quantity, or even repetitive, production. The second carving exactly like its predecessor begins to tax my patience, and

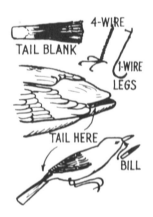

Fig. 25. Details of assembly.

Figs. 26–27. Blocky and crude wrens were my early efforts at stylizing.

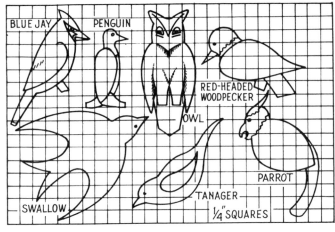

Fig. 28. I sold many of these miniatures, carved and painted, during the Depression.

Fig. 29. Silhouettes for seven birds. To make a pin or pendant, use ¼-in (6.4-mm) squares in copying. For a hand-size bird, use ½- or ¾-in (12.7- or 19.2-mm) squares.

fortunately I have not had to rely upon carving, or books about it, as my basic source of income.

An easy way to start carving birds is to make miniatures perched on twigs or tiny houses on spits, to be stuck into potted plants or wherever. Such birds are so small that details are unnecessary, and won't be seen anyway; it is only necessary to get the general shape, then color the bird

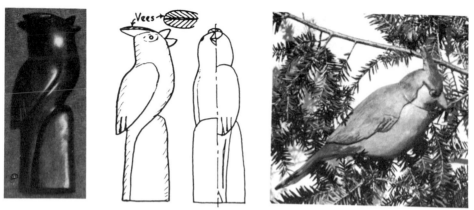

Figs. 30–31. *Cardinal in cherry, natural. Fig. 32. Female cardinal in pine, painted.*

Figs. 33–35. *From Greece comes this pair of olivewood owls, sacred to Athena. (The carver got the correct number of toes on the facing owl, but has three forward on the side-view owl.) The carver, Spyros Kokkinakes, of the island of Hydra, was famous for his owls. These are an interesting pair to try, so I have included patterns.*

Fig. 36. Life-size cedar waxwing, with wing and tail feathering, was carved by Howard D. Green of Houston, Texas, who has written two books on model birds. Note the professional mounting including driftwood and a machined base, as well as expert painting.

Figs. 37–38. From Indonesia come these three birds carved integral with their bases. They are 4 in (10.2 cm) high, in a very hard, dark-red wood, with red-jewel eyes.

Note: Indonesian and Malaysian carvers tend to combine a bird with its supporting base. See Chapter V.

Fig. 39. Monolithic and stylized, this life-size duck was in the window of a Jogjakarta, Java, shop. The entire body is fine-lined for texture, with a few ruffled wing and tail feathers projecting. Eyes are carved, not glass.

Fig. 40. With a spotted red body and exaggerated wings and tail, this carved goose is a decoration in a rural Balinese restaurant. It is larger than life and brilliantly colored.

Fig. 41. Typical of many miniatures now available at reasonable prices, this redhead duck, about 4 in (10.2 cm) long, has wing and tail feathering carefully defined by painting. Edward Clist of New Jersey was the carver.

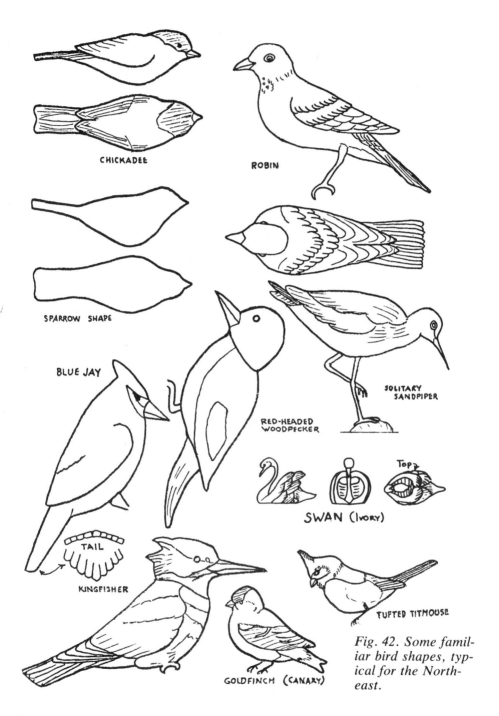

CHICKADEE

ROBIN

SPARROW SHAPE

BLUE JAY

RED-HEADED WOODPECKER

SOLITARY SANDPIPER

SWAN (IVORY)

Top

TAIL

KINGFISHER

TUFTED TITMOUSE

GOLDFINCH (CANARY)

Fig. 42. Some familiar bird shapes, typical for the Northeast.

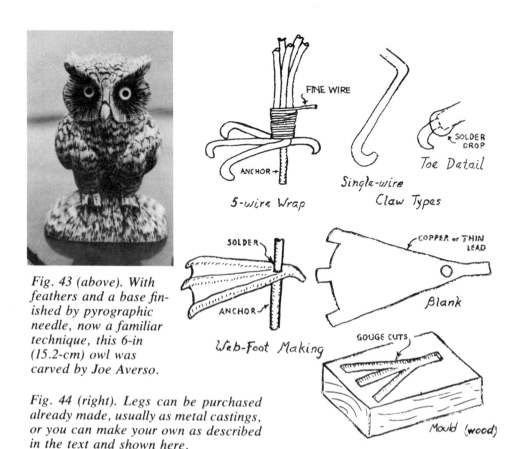

FINE WIRE

ANCHOR →

5-wire Wrap

Single-wire
Claw Types

SOLDER
DROP

Toe Detail

SOLDER

ANCHOR

Web-Foot Making

COPPER or THIN
LEAD

Blank

GOUGE CUTS

Mould (wood)

Fig. 43 (above). With feathers and a base finished by pyrographic needle, now a familiar technique, this 6-in (15.2-cm) owl was carved by Joe Averso.

Fig. 44 (right). Legs can be purchased already made, usually as metal castings, or you can make your own as described in the text and shown here.

appropriately with bright, solid colors. In the late twenties and early thirties, I made many of these from such scraps as I had; they could be sold for pennies—and I needed pennies to supplement a fading Depression salary.

When your birds exceed an inch or so in length, pay attention to pose, head shape, tail position and the like. I have sketched some familiar birds so you can see characteristic silhouettes. If you prefer some other bird, start with a picture, or several pictures, that provide full side views, and have the head aligned with the body, not turned. Or carve the body and head separately, and mate the two, as I did with the Canada goose, setting the rough-shaped head at a suitable angle when you glue, then shaping the neck to suit.

In birds, it is essential to get the proper silhouette, although several

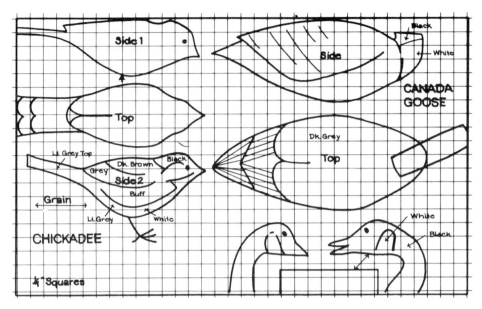

CANADA GOOSE

Side 1 · Top · Side · Black · White

Dk. Grey · Top

Lt. Grey Top · Dk. Brown · Black · Grey · Dk Grey · Side 2 · Buff · Grain · Lt Grey · White

CHICKADEE

¼" Squares

White · Black

Figs. 45–47. Canada goose, chickadee and scarlet tanager with detailed patterns. The chickadee is almost life-size, and the tanager is made from a similar blank. These birds show major wing and tail lines only, and are painted with oils. The Canada goose has more feather detail in both carving and painting.

28

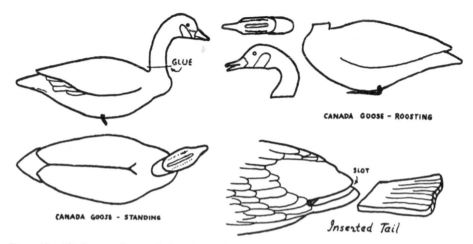

Fig. 48. Slight angling of the Canada-goose head enlivens the model. Spread wings and tails are best carved separately and inserted.

species of birds can be carved from a block of a similar silhouette, like warblers and canaries, blue jays and cardinals, or even sparrows and chickadees. Obviously, the owl, the flamingo, the goose and some other birds have very distinctive silhouettes that should be exploited in your carving.

Primitive carvers tend to stress the silhouette, or perhaps to overstress it, and this is not bad, within reason. Someone who makes a portrait of you does the same thing—he stresses your peculiarities. However, if he over-does it, the portrait becomes a caricature. The same thing is true of birds. Bird sculptors tend to stress flight rather than static pose, streamlining rather than detail. They do not add accessories, and tend to tone rather than color—if they use color at all. They carve hard woods and may be careful not to fight the grain by overdetailing.

The easiest woods to work for simple bird models are basswood, jelutong, white pine, willow, alder, and the like. Even balsa can be shaped into decoys. It is possible to use Styrofoam™ and papier mâché on decoys. Patterns are in bird guides, carving books, nature magazines, children's posters and Audubon prints.

Sketch the bird to the size you want, enlarging or reducing by the method of squares (draw a matrix to cover the source, and another larger or smaller matrix by the degree of change; for example, ⅛-in [3.2-mm] squares on the subject, ¼-in [6.4-mm] squares on the wood to double the

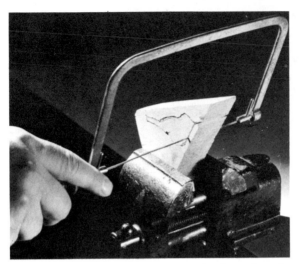

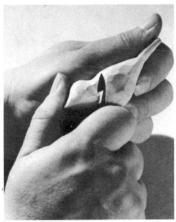

Fig. 49. Step I in carving any bird is the sil-houette. Here I am cutting a wren blank with a coping saw. (I put the blade in so it cuts on the pull stroke, as the Japanese do.)

Fig. 50. Step II is whittling the shape. Grain should run from head to tail. Small blanks can be hand-held, but watch out for your human vise!

size or ⅟₁₆-in [1.6-mm] squares to halve it). Saw out the blank with a coping or band saw. It is easier to make elements like spread tails and opened wings separately and with favorable grain, then glue them into place, into a slot if necessary.

The bill is easier as a separate element, particularly if it is across grain. The tail may also be, if it is a sharp angle to the line of the body. Legs can have many forms. I have used brads stuck into a hole in the base, with the toes delineated in the base wood. Another bird was presumably on a limb or block, so its legs did not show at all. I have made birds with an alnico magnet set into the body so they would cling to a refrigerator door or a firescreen. The usual form for songbirds is a toed leg, which I have made by winding a small-diameter wire around four other wires that become claws. The wire can also be wound around five wires, which leaves one to go straight down for entry into the base.

For larger birds, like the predators, you may want to shape thighs for the upper legs, and drill them to take the wire lower legs and feet. It is also possible to make feet by soldering on a separate foot of wire or cut metal, leaving a small blob of solder at the center to form the claw pad.

For webbed feet, make a mould by cutting gouge lines of the proper

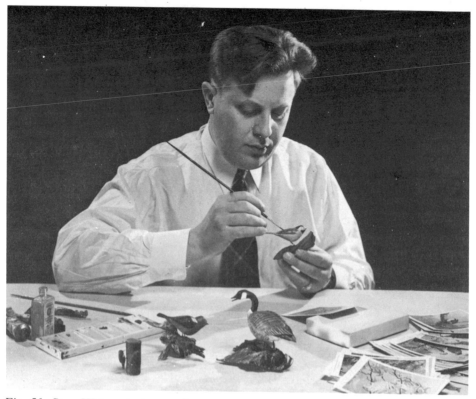

Fig. 51. Step III is painting—unless you want to sand the carving; I usually don't. When I paint, I have pictures to consult, and use oil pigments with drier or varnish. (This picture was taken 40 years ago—ah, me!)

length, and angle intaglio in a block. Then form a thin sheet of copper or lead into the mould by hammering or pressing with a pad. The resulting foot can be filed to shape and drilled for soldering to a leg wire or wires. Also, the leg can be shaped by adding plastic wood, solder or clay over the support wire.

Second only to decoys in popularity is the eagle. It is so popular, in fact, that there is at least one book devoted to patterns for it, and some entrepreneurs offer patterns or even blanks and instructions. I have devoted a separate chapter to it. You can also find eagle patterns on almost any federal building, on stock certificates and even on coins.

CHAPTER IV

Tops in Model Birds

Fig. 52. Snowy owl by Charles Chase is 22 in (55.9 cm) tall, in elm. The figure is monolithic, although claws barely touch the base. No feathering is indicated and wing edges are smooth. Eyes are simply rounded hollows with a central pillar. Note the base "pool."

Fig. 53. Green heron 19 in (48.3 cm) tall, carved in one piece from olivewood by Charles G. "Chippy" Chase of Brunswick, Maine. The wood has a greenish tone and decided figure. There is no feather delineation, no glass eyes, no added legs. Mouth and eye positions are only suggested. There is some texturing of the feet. The freestanding water-plant leaf is characteristic of the carver's style.

Fig. 54. Grainger McCoy of Wadmallow Island, South Carolina, here is assembling a red-shouldered hawk attacking a copperhead snake. The life-size bird is supported only by its left claw. Feathers are individual or in small groups, textured and tinted by pyrographic needle and oil paints.

Fig. 55. Companion red-shouldered hawk attacks the snake from the side. (It is at upper right of its companion.) It is cantilevered out from one claw so delicately that it trembles when visitors pass. Feather technique is evident here. Mr. McCoy worked with Gilbert Maggioni of Beaufort, South Carolina, for several years, and these birds were a combined effort shown in New York in 1974.

CHAPTER V

The Birds of Bali

Based on triangles rather than rectangles, they support fragile parts

WHILE BALI AND THE UNITED STATES are alike in their emphasis on birds as subjects for carving, the similarity stops right there. The emphasis in the United States has been on realism, on producing carvings of birds that look as much as possible like the real thing, because it is a challenge to produce such a carving and because the finished product, if well-made and particularly if produced by a known carver, commands a premium from collectors. The decoys we carve will never descend to attracting mere ducks; they are masterpieces of carving and painting—at least the best ones are.

In contrast, the Balinese birds are, with very few exceptions, not

Figs. 56–57. Small ducks with topknot are common sights in Bali. Note the variation in presumably the same pose (see Fig. 59, next page). The dark ducks are macassar ebony, the light ones a wood like our maple. The wing-extended bird is about 7 in (17.8 cm) tall and illustrates the triangular basis of many Balinese birds.

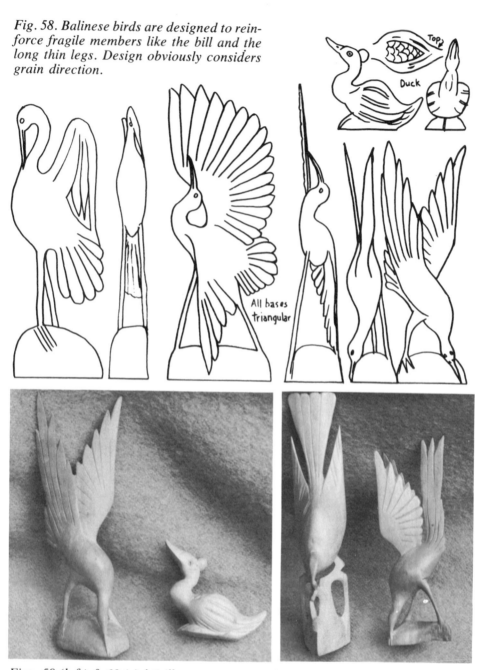

Fig. 58. Balinese birds are designed to rein-
force fragile members like the bill and the
long thin legs. Design obviously considers
grain direction.

Duck

TOP?

All bases
triangular

Figs. 59 (left) & 60 (right) illustrate grace and apparent delicacy.

Fig. 61 (left). These ebony pieces have the triangular cross section that utilizes grain for strength. The central figure is complex but sturdy because of the supporting branches (see Fig. 63). Fig. 62 (right). An in-the-round ebony eagle on an orb is an unusual shape for Bali.

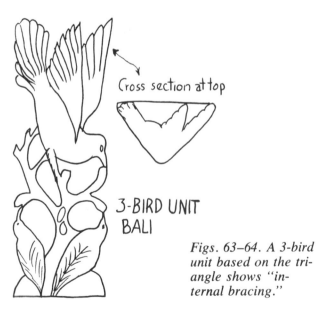

Cross section at top

3-BIRD UNIT
BALI

Figs. 63–64. A 3-bird unit based on the triangle shows "internal bracing."

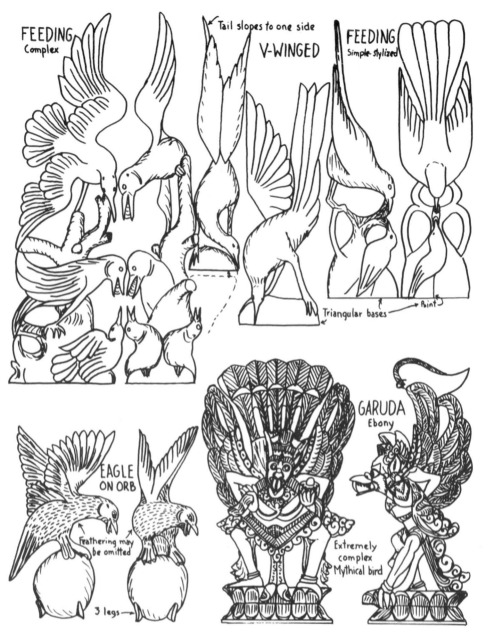

FEEDING
Complex

Tail slopes to one side
V-WINGED

FEEDING
Simple-stylized

Triangular bases   Point

EAGLE
ON ORB

Feathering may
be omitted

3 legs →

GARUDA
Ebony

Extremely
complex
Mythical bird

Fig. 65. Traditional Balinese carving like the Garuda at lower right was religious in many instances, and very detailed. Modern work like the birds has adapted itself to stylizing and elimination of detail.

Figs. 66–68. Garudas (bird demons helpful to man) are the chosen vehicle of Vishnu and typical of traditional Balinese carving. The detail and complexity can be appreciated by comparing Figs. 66 & 67 (top left and right) with Figs. 65 & 68. The 2-ft (61-cm) tall painted one is an assembly, but the 7½-in (19.1-cm) ebony one is monolithic, yet full of pierced carving and design detail—too much to show even in the sketch.

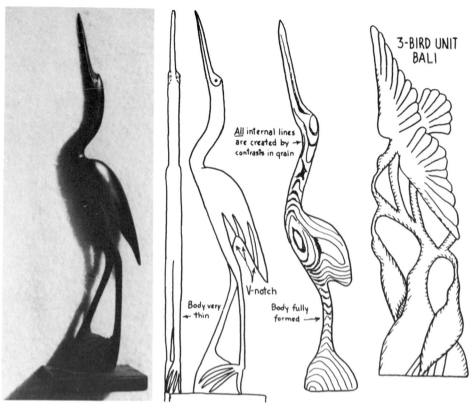

All internal lines
are created by
contrasts in grain

V-notch

Body very
← thin

Body fully
formed →

3-BIRD UNIT
BALI

Figs. 69–70. The attenuated figure of a flamingo, once common, is now rare in Bali. The American flamingo with it is designed for production.

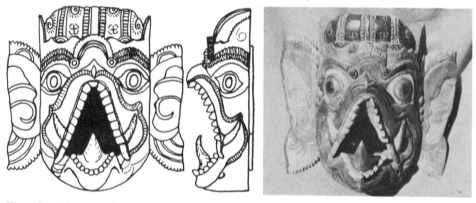

Figs. 71–72. Garuda bird-god mask, worn by an actor, is painted soft wood. Ears and other elements may be added. Note the carving detail.

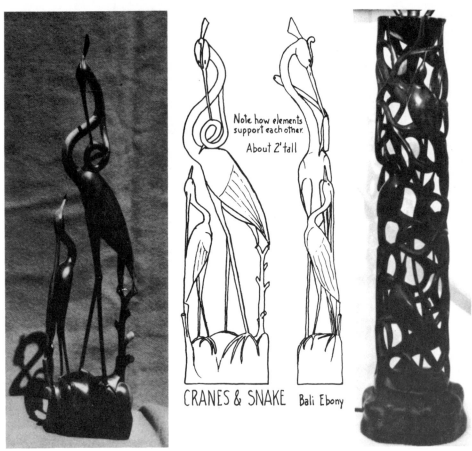

Note how elements support each other.

About 2' tall

CRANES & SNAKE   Bali Ebony

Figs. 73 (left) & 74 (center). Intricacy and apparent fragility are illustrated by this combination of cranes with a snake. Actually, the snake helps protect the beak of one crane, while long crest feathers support that of the other. Spindly legs of both birds are reinforced by stumps.

painted; they are primarily carved in good woods left visible by clear finishing. More importantly, they are stylized, designed not for ver-isimilitude but for decoration and utility. Thus, the typical carving is not rectangular, and such fragile elements as legs and beak are designed with some support so they won't be damaged by dusting. Furthermore, they are in macassar ebony or an equally hard, lighter colored wood, for which the United States has no equivalent combining color and workability. (In the United States, there is a choice between walnut, maple and holly.)

Thus, the Balinese excel in carving stylized bird figures that have an

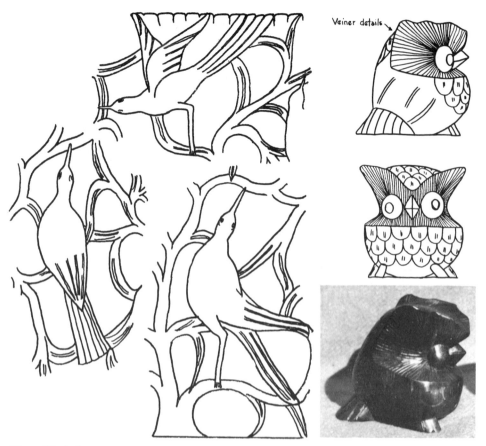

Figs. 75 (left) & 76 (above). This macassar-ebony lampbase is 3½ in × 19 in (8.9 cm × 48.3 cm) tall. Birds and vines support each other. Figs. 77–78 (above right). Designed by Ida Bagus Tilem, this owl is squat and fat in ebony, with high stylization.

innate grace but are quite sturdy. However, the typical Balinese carver uses small tools (without handles) and a club instead of a mallet, so he takes many small cuts instead of fewer larger ones. He is not concerned with time as we are. As a result, he can produce delicate legs and beaks without breakage, although most of the designs I've seen are conscious of grain and the necessity of support for a long projection. This results in beaks and legs supported by twining vines or branches.

Beyond that, the Balinese are basically more aesthetic—which may or may not be a virtue. They are also more effeminate, which results in carvings that may offend macho American males. However, they attract the American female as few other carvings do.

While the tendency in the United States is to design and carve pieces that are rectangular in cross section, Balinese birds tend to be triangular. This shape is probably easier to split from a log without wasting wood, yet the carvings have the necessary stability. Designs are, of course, adjusted to the cross section. Also, there seem to be a series of basic shapes that are carved, but no two of the same general design will be exactly alike.

This method of carving is a real achievement, and results in the necessity for the buyer to pick and choose, which is not a problem here.

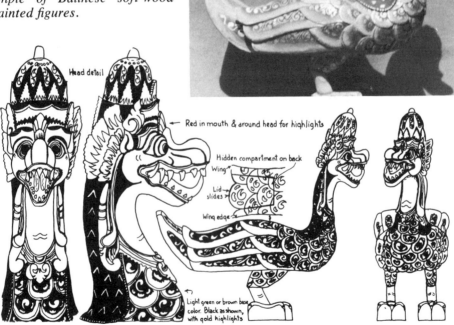

Figs. 79–80. The Bebek dragon duck, life-size, has considerable carving detail around the head, supplemented by painted detail elsewhere. He has a hidden compartment in his back for prayers and offerings in temple worship. He is an excellent example of Balinese soft-wood painted figures.

Head detail

← Red in mouth & around head for highlights

Hidden compartment on back
Wing
Lid
slides
Wing edge

Light green or brown base color. Black as shown, with gold highlights

CHAPTER VI

The Stylized Bird—or Is It?

There is a difference between stylized and crude

"STYLIZED" IS, I FEAR, a word that covers a great many sins. Whenever a bird carving is distorted, anatomically incorrect or just plain crude, one explanation may be that it is "stylized." But the term, properly used, means something in which the dimensions have been altered *intentionally* to create a pattern or make the object conform to a style of expression or a convention rather than to nature. It is *not* an excuse for bad design.

Many primitive carvings are stylized for one reason or another: to suit a religious theme; to permit their embodiment in a decorative plan; to enable them to be used as an element of something else; or to symbolize the feeling of the carver or the beliefs of his people. One man's stylizing may be another's caricature or cartoon. Thus, the examples I have selected here may not fit your definition of stylizing—but even if they do not, they are different—and interesting.

Stylizing can be quite straightforward and simple, or extremely complicated. I have been particularly conscious of the effect of stylizing in relief carving, and have discussed that in Chapter XII. Just as a child creates an airplane by crossing one stick over another, or a horse by having a head on a stick, you or I can stylize—or claim to have stylized—something as we will. I have included a number of examples of stylized birds from foreign countries, as well as from the United States, that will underscore this.

Figs. 81–83. The owl is recognizable almost regardless of how he is carved. Here are three examples, one a standard neckerchief slide, the second with feathering and details picked out by burning with a pyrographic needle, and the third a bit of pine branch with a pointed bill inserted. They come from Oregon, New Hampshire and New Mexico, respectively.

Figs. 84 (top left) & 87 (left). A New Mexico carver of santos made this cedar tree of birds and the two birds below it. All are intentionally angular.

Fig. 85 (top center). Easter Island birds, the longer being 6 in (15.2 cm). The first is simply a stylized bird, but the second recalls the birdman culture there.

Figs. 86 (top right) & 88 (left). Mexican stylizations.

Figs. 89–90 (bottom). For a child, I carved a barn complete with its denizens. Figures were pine. Here are ducks and chickens, the tallest 1 in (2.5 cm). Fledglings are grouped on panels.

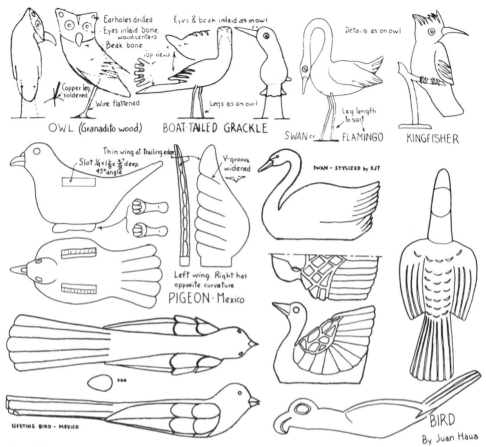

Fig. 91. From Guerrero, Mexico, come the stylized (almost caricatured) birds at top, as well as the contrasting examples at left, one expertly made (Fig. 93, next page), the other a novice's product (Fig. 92). The center sketch is the swan of Fig. 88, compared with a more formal one of mine. The bird at lower right is from Easter Island (see Fig. 85).

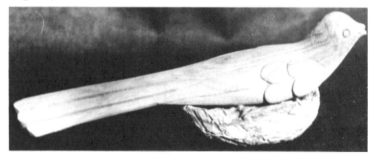

Fig. 92. Bird with nest and eggs carved in blanco. It is about 8 in (20.3 cm) long.

Fig. 93. Experimental rendition of a dove in mesquite, 6 in (15.2 cm) long, with wings carved separately and inserted (Fig. 92), proved to be too expensive to produce in quantity, so was abandoned in Mexico.

Fig. 94 (above right). Hen in grey marble, carved in France by Ed M. Sandoz, has expert stylizing, worthy of careful study.

Fig. 95 (left). Miniature birds provide inexpensive purchases for "browsers" at shows. The snipe is from New York, the quail by a Seri in Mexico.

Figs. 96 (far left) & 97. These birds suggest the range of stylizing. One is a 3D water bird silhouette from Texas, the other a maple duckling from North Carolina. The duckling is much more detailed.

Figs. 98 (top left) & 100 (above). Here are a duck in grey slate from Labrador, about 8 in (20.3 cm) long, and two cormorant carvings from King Island, Alaska, the taller one 4½ in (11.4 cm). They are mastodon ivory, and the pair are mounted on a whale vertebra.

Figs. 99 (top right) & 101 (above). An Eskimo blank (see Fig. 129) from which I whittled the walrus-ivory duck. The oils-tinted puffins are mounted on the same walrus-tusk butt from which they are carved.

The key point in stylizing is to have a reason, or to desire an effect. It is not enough to carve something, and when you realize that it is out of proportion, claim it is stylized. At that point, it is just an experiment that failed. On the other hand, if you have created something that makes your point, and strongly, you may have a legitimate stylized piece, primitive as

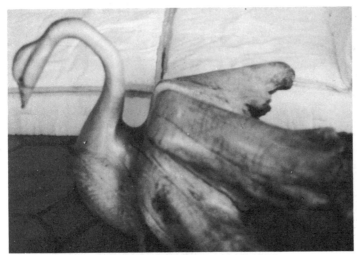

Fig. 102. Don't forget that a natural shape can become a carving with a little help. This 30-in (76.2-cm) swan carved from a mesquite stump was in a Scottsdale, Arizona, store window.

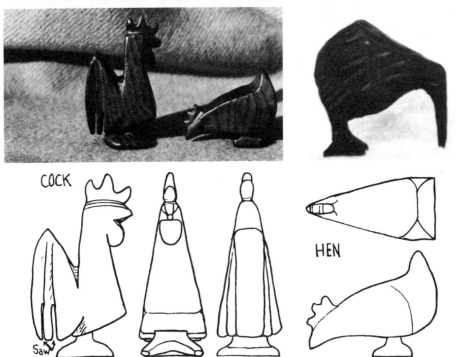

Figs. 103–105. From the Argentine came the cock and hen above, while the kiwi (Fig. 104, upper right) is from Australia. They are in strong-grained soft woods, stained black, a common finish among primitives. These figures are easy.

Figs. 106–107 (right). Somewhat sophisticated parakeet from Greek Isles, carved with a rotary tool which burned the soft white wood to create contrast and color.

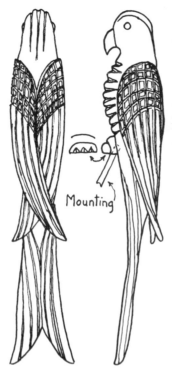

Figs. 108–109 (below). This bird is a modern copy of a prehistoric design from Paracas, Peru, but carved in a piece of house-support post, also prehistoric. The design is simple but strong, and the finish is black stain.

Mounting

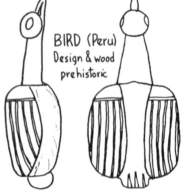

BIRD (Peru)
Design & wood prehistoric

it may be. The final judgment in such matters is for local authorities, I suppose, who may or may not know the difference. As Steinberg once said about a carved caricature, "If it sells, it is art!"

Birds are, I suppose, a natural subject for stylizing, because they play such a familiar part in our daily lives. In many countries, they have also been involved with religion. The Maori and other Polynesians believed a bird carried the god Pourangahua to New Zealand. Easter Islanders had their birdman gods. Papua New Guinea incorporated the sea eagle in its

49

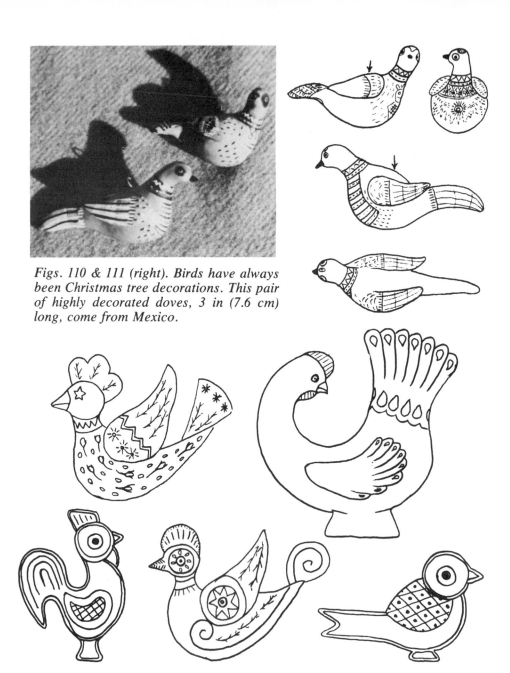

Figs. 110 & 111 (right). Birds have always been Christmas tree decorations. This pair of highly decorated doves, 3 in (7.6 cm) long, come from Mexico.

Fig. 112. Similar Christmas tree birds come from European countries. They can be cut from ⅛-in (3.2-mm) wood or made 3D. Length is 3 in (7.6 cm).

PARROT - U.S.S.R. - HORN

FACE

TAIL

Figs. 113–115 (above & right). Limitations in horn shape have led to some interesting birds. Here are examples from the USSR and Penang, Malaysia (center in photo). They are 6 in (15.2 cm) tall.

Fig. 116 (below). Swan in ivory in the classical pose. It is 1 in (2.5 cm) long, and carved in Germany many years ago.

TOP of HEAD
NOTE TILT to LEFT

SIDE of HEAD

LEGS
SAWED
& BENT

SHORE BIRD - U.S.S.R. HORN

CRANE - PENANG - HORN

Fig. 117. Two horn birds from India. The flat swan is 5 in (12.7 cm) long.

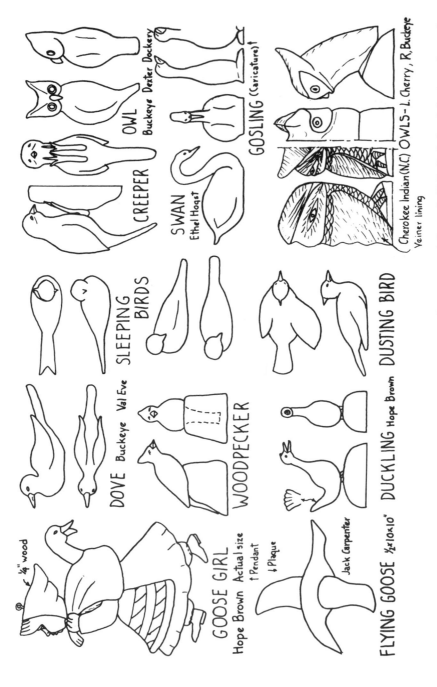

OWL
Buckeye Dexter Dockery

GOSLING (Caricature)↑

(Cherokee Indian(N.C.) OWLS – L. Cherry, R. Buckeye
Veiner lining

CREEPER

SWAN
Ethel Hoast

SLEEPING
BIRDS

DUSTING BIRD

DOVE Buckeye Val Eve

WOODPECKER

DUCKLING Hope Brown

¼" wood

GOOSE GIRL
Hope Brown Actual size
↑ Pendant
↓ Plaque

Jack Carpenter

FLYING GOOSE ½×10×10"

Fig. 118. Stylizing can take many forms. Some are shown in these typical Campbell Folk School designs (see also the duckling, Fig. 120). The two very different owls are by nearby Cherokee Indians. All are carved in native woods and have a clear finish to show grain.

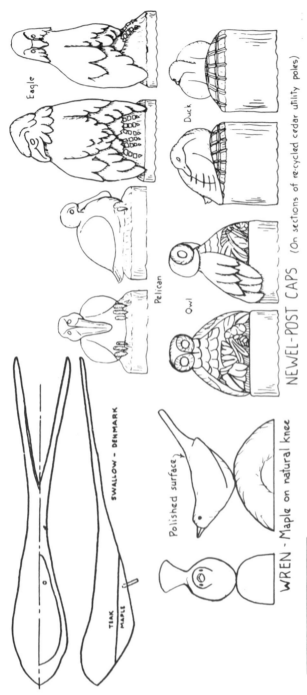

Eagle

Duck

Pelican

Owl

NEWEL-POST CAPS (On sections of recycled cedar utility poles)

SWALLOW – DENMARK

TEAK

MAPLE

Polished surface

WREN – Maple on natural knee

Fig. 119 (above). Newel-post caps, carved by tyros for Timberline Lodge, Oregon, from discarded cedar poles in 1937, are at right. At left is a Danish swallow and a wren from New Hampshire. Fig. 120 (left). Indignant duckling. Fig. 121 (right). These greatly enlongated Danish swallows are laminates of teak and maple, set on a nest block of African wood.

53

Feathering detailed, prominent

Legs & feet oversize, not textured

Fig. 122 (left). Rooster 35 in (88.9 cm) tall, carved by Mato Generalic of Yugoslavia. Fig. 123 (above). Hen from Costa Rica, shown full size. Figs. 124–125 (below). Parrot 14 in (35.6 cm) tall in nawa nawa wood from Fiji.

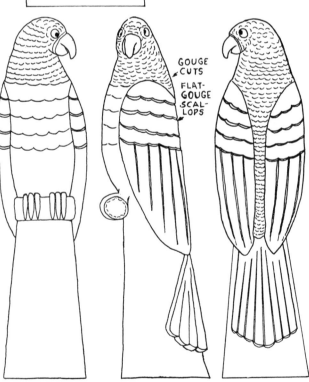

GOUGE CUTS

FLAT-GOUGE SCALLOPS

Figs. 126–127 (right). This warbler, 4 in (10.2 cm) high including base, was carved in mahogany in our Southern Highlands. It is exemplary in its simplicity and integration with its base. Note that it avoids the problems of legs and feathering without loss.

Yellow

Orange

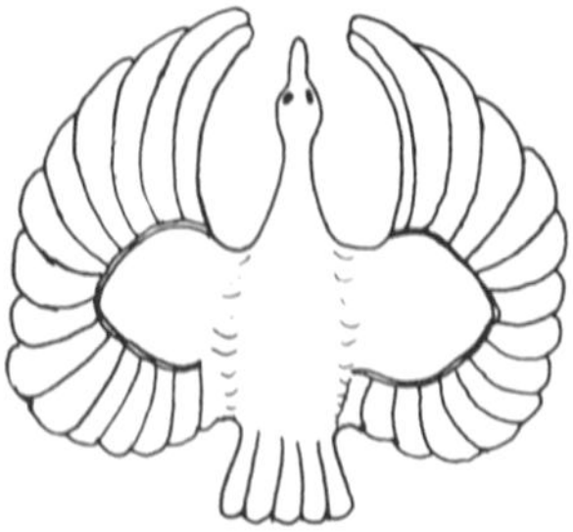

Figs. 128 (above) & 129 (right). Patterns for puffins (Fig. 99) and a flying duck (Fig. 101). The duck is a pendant, almost flat.

coat of arms; the United States uses the bald eagle. Germany and Russia included eagles in their imperial coats of arms. Mexico has the eagle, snake and cactus. All of these were stylized sooner or later.

It is not only the mighty birds that play a part in history and tradition. Americans put ornaments of small birds on their Christmas trees. Tales are told of geese that saved a city, of birds that carried messages, of birds that carried men. Aesop and other tale tellers wove stories around them, stylizing in words. Pioneers and farmers have carved birds for their children; sculptors have carved them for high altars and cathedrals. The examples here are really modest in the light of tradition, but they have been selected because they are easy to carve in most cases, and are quite different from other birds illustrated in this book. Many can be made with the knife alone in soft wood.

CHAPTER VII

The Stylizing Seris of Sonora

A short story of a craft that became a power factory

ABOUT 20 YEARS AGO, JOSÉ ASTORGA, a Seri Indian in Sonora, Mexico, began to sell his simple carvings in the local ironwood (*Olney tesota*). This convinced the whole tribe to switch from basketmaking to woodcarving, using machetes to rough out the pieces, rasps to shape them and even motor oil to polish them. The peculiarity of the pieces is that they are not primitive in the usual sense, but highly stylized and almost sophisticated. Their design complements the wood, and the smooth polish gives them an attractive glow, so they sold readily to Americans.

When the *mestizos* saw this success, they set up a factory with power tools in Hermosillo and supplied "Seri" carvings to stores all over the country at low prices. So the Seri Indians are not carving much anymore; they've gone back to weaving baskets, except for José's daughter, Aurora, who is now the best Seri carver, and a few others. It's a pity.

Figs. 130–131 (above). Stylized flying eagle with 14-in (35.6-cm) wingspread. Note head shape in side view. Fig. 132 (right). A 12-in (30.5-cm) standing eagle. Later designs leave the base rough.

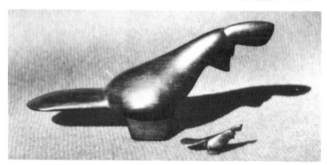

Fig. 133 (above left). California quail and owl, the latter 12 in (30.5 cm) tall. Fig. 134 (above right). Pelican 8 in (20.3 cm) tall, and eaglet 6 in (15.2 cm) tall. Note rough bases, contrasting with smooth finish of the birds. Fig. 135 (mid-right). Two sizes of California quail, the smaller 1 in (2.5 cm) long, the larger 7 in (17.8 cm).

Fig. 136 (right). Duck and road runner 18 in (45.7 cm) long. Eyes and feathers are not defined (except for the owl, Fig. 133).

CHAPTER VIII

Some "Special" Birds

Articulated pieces, combinations, fetishes and other ideas

THREE-DIMENSIONAL AND RELIEF-CARVED birds are quite familiar; less so are the special carvings, such as birds incorporated in some other design, panel scene or a totem pole, articulated birds, wood shapes that suggest birds, and the like. There are tribes in Africa and Borneo that worship the hornbill and make effigies of this bird. There are Mexican carvers who achieve bird designs on an inexpensive soft-wood wedding chest by making an outline of triangular incisions, something like spaced chip carving. The possibilities are endless, and I can show only a few of them here.

The Northwest Coast Indians made totem poles often topped by an eagle or a raven, both familiar birds in that area, and considered powerful totems. They also made dance masks of them. The bird was interpreted by

Figs. 137–138. Articulated pine owl, unpainted, from the USSR, is a wall hanger.

Fig. 139. From the Mahakam River come these two Dayak hornbill depictions. The lower was carved from a log and set atop a post; each hornbill is 12 ft (3.7 m) long. The 6-ft (1.83-m) upper is less primitive, and the African fetish smaller.

Note: Birds color the beliefs of many peoples. The hornbill, slow-flying, big and ungainly, has a close connection with the Creation in Dayak (Borneo) culture, and also occurs in African totems. The crane is a symbol in Japan, etc.

Fig. 141. The crane symbolizes long life in Japan. Here a pair is scrimshanded into a water-buffalo horn scene. (The smaller horn, from Okinawa, depicts a medieval castle.)

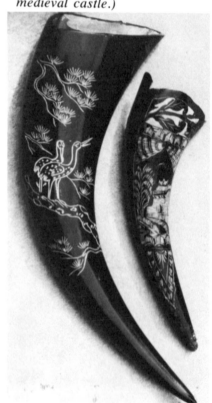

Fig. 140 (above). Owl's wings rise when something is hung on the hook, and fall of their own weight when the hook is cleared.

Fig. 142. Three Navajo animal fetishes of stone, surrounded by a necklace with carved birds in stone, coral and abalone shell.

Fig. 144 (below). A scrap of walrus ivory suggested to me this 3-in (7.6-cm) goose flying on a piano wire over an ivory cat-tail. Base is iron-wood.

Fig. 143 (left). Europe has its legends about birds, too. Probably best known is the Brementown Musicians. This is my copy of the bronze statue before the Rathaus in Bremen, West Germany. The walnut panel is 1 × 12½ × 20 in (2.5 × 31.8 × 50.8 cm).

Figs. 145–146. Northwest Coast Indians made much of the eagle and the raven, first in dance masks, later in totem poles. Here are examples of both. The bird is often so stylized that it is unidentifiable to the layman.

Fig. 147. Totem pole with birds awake. *Fig. 148. Totem pole with birds asleep.*

Fig. 149. Northwest Coast Indians carved "grease bowls" in stone or wood in which a wick of moss or cloth floated in whale or bear oil. This made a crude lamp. Hugh C. Minton, Jr. carved this copy.

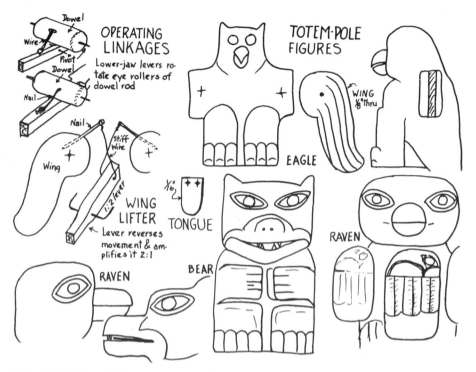

OPERATING LINKAGES

Dowel

Wire

Pivot Dowel

Nail

Nail

Lower-jaw levers rotate eye rollers of dowel rod

Stiff Wire

Wing

WING LIFTER

1:2 lever

Lever reverses movement & amplifies it 2:1

TONGUE

⅛"

RAVEN

BEAR

TOTEM-POLE FIGURES

WING ⅛" thru

EAGLE

RAVEN

Fig. 150. This miniature totem pole is articulated so the eagle at top raises his wings, and both eagle and raven, as well as the base bear, open their eyes when a rear lever is pressed. Raven and eagle designs are copied directly from an old totem pole, not from the newer chain-sawed versions.

the particular carver, so was usually highly stylized, sometimes to such a degree as to be unrecognizable to an outsider. Various primitives have carved birds, sometimes just because a particular piece of driftwood suggested a wing or body shape, sometimes merely as a toy for the children. I have never been particularly interested in carving precise copies of the birds around me, but have, ever since I can remember, carved and whittled variations based on a piece of wood or an oddball idea. Some of these are shown elsewhere in this book. Some are here. Some, mercifully, are gone without record.

The point is that it can be fun to make what you choose to call a bird, whether or not it is obvious, or likeable, or good art to the observer. It gives you a little opportunity to be free of the limitations of earth.

CHAPTER IX

Birds Can Be Caricatured

Some are unintentional, but all should provoke a smile

CARICATURE IN A SENSE IS merely exaggerated portraiture: The personal peculiarities of the subject are emphasized in portraiture, overemphasized in caricature. Thus, in many instances, woodcarvers attempting a portrait overdo it, and achieve caricature. This is particularly evident in so many "portraits" of Lincoln (thin face, warts), Kennedy (fatter face, bouffant hairdo) and now of Reagan. It can also occur with portraits of animals, but our knowledge of animal anatomy is so much more limited that we often don't notice.

Then there is the intentional caricature, of which perhaps the owl is the most obvious victim. This bird has a reputation for sagacity, but the

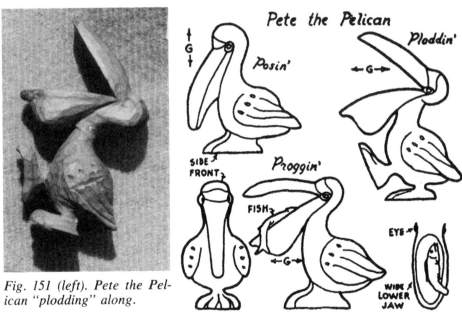

Fig. 151 (left). Pete the Pelican "plodding" along.

Fig. 152 (right). Fifty years ago, I wrote for Popular Mechanics about carving Pete the Pelican. He is a simple figure, and distortion improves the caricature.

Figs. 153–154. This basswood owl I carved during the Depression to grace the peak of a rich son's shack. His father felt that my $5 charge was high! It is a 12-in (30.5-cm) caricature with too many forward toes.

Figs. 155–156. Pre-sawed blanks always tempt me to carve something other than the intended figure. These blanks are ostensibly for owls, but I carved them double-sided, so they're owls on one face, but a catbird and a cowbird on the other. The cowbird head has a copper nose ring. Patterns on next page.

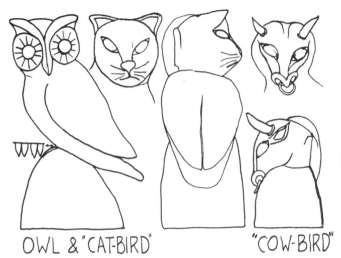

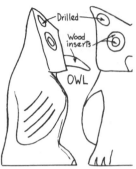

OWL & "CAT-BIRD"   "COW-BIRD"

Fig. 157. Patterns for owls of Figs. 155–156.

Fig. 158. Guerrero, Mexico, was the source of this owl with inserted eyes and bill, and drilled "ears," 6 in (15.2 cm) tall.

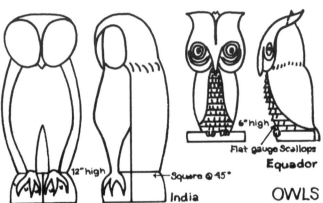

OWLS

Fig. 159 (above). Everybody caricatures owls—and differently. Here are examples from Mexico (left) and Ecuador.

Figs. 160 (above right) & 161 (right). Owl pendants in ivory (with a wink!) and in wood. The ivory one is scrimshanded and filled with India ink.

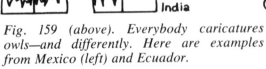

OWL PENDANT

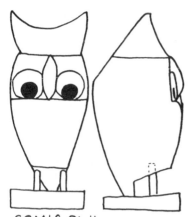

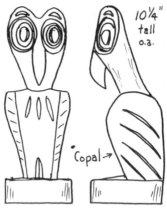

COMIC OWL Japan Cedar
Plastic inserted eyes have rolling pupils

10¼" tall o.a.

·Copal→

Figs. 163 (above) & 164 (right). Mexican owl.

Figs. 162 (above left) & 165 (left). Machine-made rolling eyes are mounted on this Japanese owl in cryptomeria, the cypress-cedar that is sandblasted to show growth rings.

Figs. 166 (right) & 167 (below). In the San Blas Islands off Panama, I bought the upper mandible of a toucan, then carved a walnut caricature to fit it. Available wood was 2¾ in (7.0 cm) thick, but he is 16 in (40.6 cm) tall!

TORO TOUCAN
Walnut, tinted. 2¾×6×16"

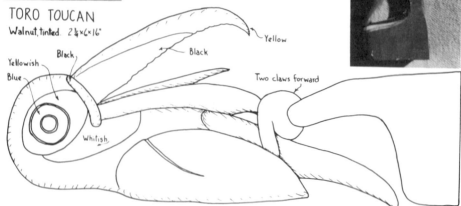

Yellow

Black

Black

Two claws forward

Yellowish

Blue

Whitish

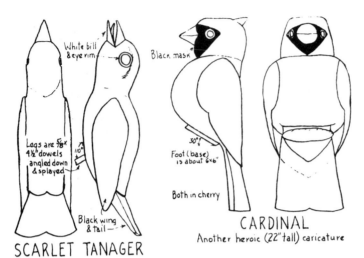

White bill & eye rim

Legs are ⅝"× 4½" dowels angled down & splayed 110°

Black wing & tail

SCARLET TANAGER
A heroic (24" tall) caricature

Black mask

30°
Foot (base) is about 6×6"

Both in cherry

CARDINAL
Another heroic (22" tall) caricature

Fig. 168 (left). Atop my "bug tree" I had a flat cardinal 22 in (55.9 cm) tall in cherry. He rotted, so I replaced him with a cherry scarlet tanager 24 in (61.0 cm) tall. But the tanager isn't as good a caricature.

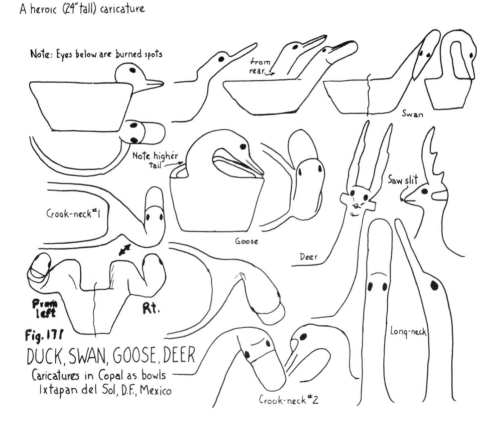

Note: Eyes below are burned spots

from rear

Swan

Note higher tail

Crook-neck #1

Goose

Deer

Saw slit

From left   Rt.

Goose

long-neck

Fig. 171
DUCK, SWAN, GOOSE, DEER
Caricatures in Copal as bowls
Ixtapan del Sol, D.F., Mexico

Crook-neck #2

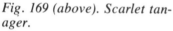

Fig. 169 (above). Scarlet tanager.

Fig. 170 (right). Typical bowls
of Fig. 171 (far lower left).

feather ruffs around his eyes and the tufts that look like ears make him a
natural clown. The long neck of the goose leads to similar treatment. One
of my friends scandalized a shop selling a standardized 15-in (38.1-cm)
goose with outstretched neck—he turned in one carving correct in every
respect except for a half-hitch (knot) in the neck, and another carving with
a neck that divided to support two heads. The shop owner put them on
display with some hesitation, and promptly sold both. Penguins are peren-
nial favorites for the caricaturist as well—including me.

Figs. 172–173. From
Sri Lanka (Ceylon)
comes this fat-
breasted dove in
ebony, 6 in (15.2 cm)
long, a wall plaque.

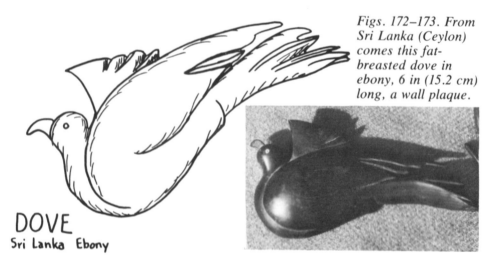

DOVE
Sri Lanka Ebony

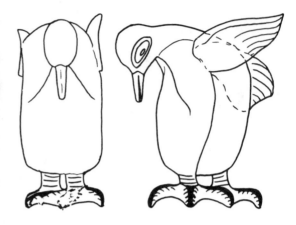

Fig. 174 (above left). Ted Haag made this emperor-penguin caricature 4 in (10.2 cm) tall. Fig. 175 (above right). A relief silhouette panel from Guatemala, this 10-in (25.4-cm) penguin contrasts with Haag's.

Fig. 176 (above). The penguin is a clown and a butt for caricature. I carved this perplexed one with one foot facing forward and the other backward. He was 6 in (15.2 cm) tall, in basswood with black tints.

Figs. 177–178. Skier penguin plaque from Ushuaia, Argentina, is 4 × 6 in (10.2 × 15.2 cm), and has pierced areas filled with tinted clear plastic.

Masks are of Nux Vomica, called "Kaderu"

HAWK (Gurula)

Fig. 180. Masks are often caricatures. This one from Sri Lanka is a fat-bodied bird with absurdly small wings.

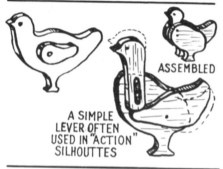

ASSEMBLED

A SIMPLE LEVER OFTEN USED IN "ACTION" SILHOUTTES

Figs. 179 (top) & 181 (above). Articulated birds usually have funny movements. At top is a Russian push toy with plywood wings that flap from wheel eccentrics. Below is a chick that bobs its head when its tail is pushed, and one with movable wings.

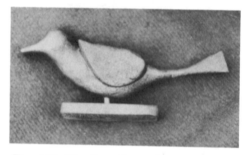

Fig. 182. The "gee" or "kiki" flies backward, with reversed wings and rudder tail "to keep the wind out of his eyes."

Caricature can serve a purpose in bird carving. It can emphasize a bird characteristic or it can produce a bird with some apparent human attribute or failing. Thus, we have such familiar birds as Donald and Dopey Duck, the chubby and merry bluebirds on get-well cards, Big Bird in Sesame Street, and half a dozen cartoon characters of one kind or another, including a road runner. Incidentally, one difference between a caricature and a cartoon is that the cartoon may be anything from less-flattering to cruel— so beware of cartoons!

I am showing here a few examples of what I consider to be bird caricatures. You may disagree, and consider some of these merely stylized, like the Korean wedding ducks in the next chapter. But don't be too sure!

CHAPTER X

The Korean Wedding Ducks

Stylized and blocky, these birds catch the eye

ACCORDING TO THE NEW YORK STORE that featured them, the Korean wedding ducks are "an ancient symbol of good luck and prosperity for the happy couple." As sold singly—and expensively—however, they were carved of soft wood and painted in gaudy colors. A friend mentioned that she liked the shape but not the coloring. I had a piece of 2 × 2¼-in (5.1 × 5.7-cm) dark-brown rosewood, so I made a pair of 8-in (20.3-cm) bodies from it, and added teak heads.

The original design had a gilt band painted just above the body, so I replaced that with an insert of ½-in (12.7-mm) beefwood on the female and

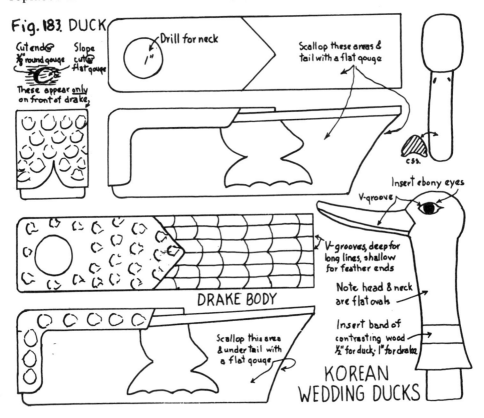

Fig. 183. DUCK

Cut ends & ⅛" round gouge

Slope cut & flat gouge

These appear only on front of drake.

Drill for neck 1"

Scallop these areas & tail with a flat gouge

c.ss.

Insert ebony eyes

V-groove

DRAKE BODY

V-grooves, deep for long lines, shallow for feather ends

Note head & neck are flat ovals

Scallop this area & under tail with a flat gouge

Insert band of contrasting wood ½" for duck; 1" for drake

KOREAN WEDDING DUCKS

Fig. 184 (top). Originals in rosewood.
Fig. 186 (above). Straight-bill loon.

Fig. 185 (top). Wenge body, maple and bubinga ring. Fig. 187 (above). Tulip body, maple, pink-ivory ring.

1-in (2.5-cm) purpleheart on the male. Eye pupils were ebony plugs. (Midway through the carving, the friend saw them and bought both.) Finishing was simply waxing, and the tassels were gilt cord glued in place.

To me, these birds appear somewhat blocky and primitive, but that seems to be part of their attraction. An interesting element is the perky and flattened head, another the stylized legs carved on the sides. The design has been so popular, in fact, that I have since made a loon and other ducks of similar pattern—all were sold before completion as well. Loons have a high "necklace" of black with white dashes, which can be suggested by an ebony insert with random V-cuts around it, into which matching V-cut slivers of holly are glued.

CHAPTER XI

Bali Bird Mobiles

Flattened and spread-winged birds catch vagrant breezes—and eyes

IN 1971, I FOUND A VERY ATTRACTIVE seabird carved of ebony in Penang, and another in Kuala Lumpur, in peninsular Malaysia. When I found a third in Singapore, I began to suspect a common origin. Although each was a bit different, all were top profiles rather than side ones, and all were macassar ebony similarly designed and carved. Further, the designs avoided long cross-grain sections and used minimum wood for the effect. Each bird was drilled with double holes at the balance point so a string could be passed through; each was a unit mobile.

Fortunately, I was travelling in the right direction; I found additional

Fig. 188. Top-profile birds, as hung in a mobile. Top whiffletree not shown.

Fig. 189. Modern top-profile birds, brightly painted, become unit mobiles. Legs are defined and painted from body back to tail on the bottom, as shown on the center bird. Wingspread is 8 in (20.3 cm).

designs and the source in Bali, and began to realize that this small island is unusual in its devotion to, and skill at, carving stylized birds. On a second visit in 1983, I saw no more of the top-profile birds; they had been succeeded by side-profile ones, except for rather gaudy painted versions of one design. But meantime, I have made and enjoyed an eight-bird mobile—and sold two half-size copies of it (with approximately 4-in [10.2-cm] birds). So here are the patterns and pictures for four designs of the new types and all eight of the old.

The older mobile is particularly sensitive to rising currents of air, such as those from a candle or heating system, while the side-profile ones are more sensitive to side drafts, of course. However, some of the side-profile ones appear to be roosting, not flying. Both types are in effect double low-relief carvings; the bodies actually bulge more than wings, and both faces

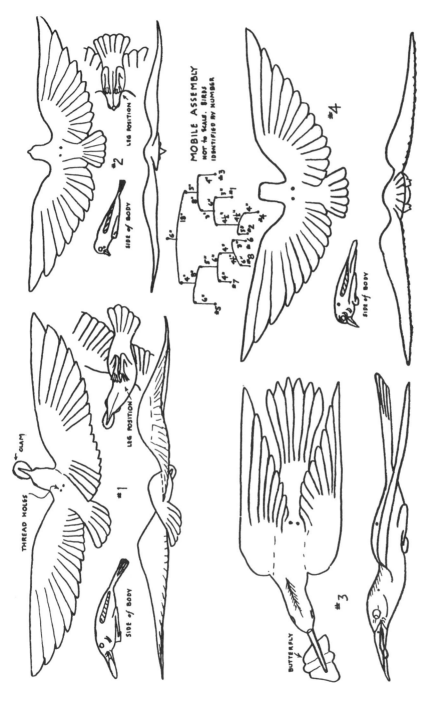

THREAD HOLES
CLAM
LEG POSITION
SIDE OF BODY
#1

LEG POSITION
SIDE OF BODY
#2

MOBILE ASSEMBLY
NOT to SCALE. BIRDS
IDENTIFIED BY NUMBER

#4
SIDE OF BODY

BUTTERFLY
#3

Figs. 190–191 (opposite page). Top-profile birds are flying, in contrast to side-profile ones (page 78). They are 8 to 9 in (20.3 to 22.8 cm) in wingspread, but flat in body. One assembly arrangement shows birds identified by number. Some have prey. Feathers are only suggested.

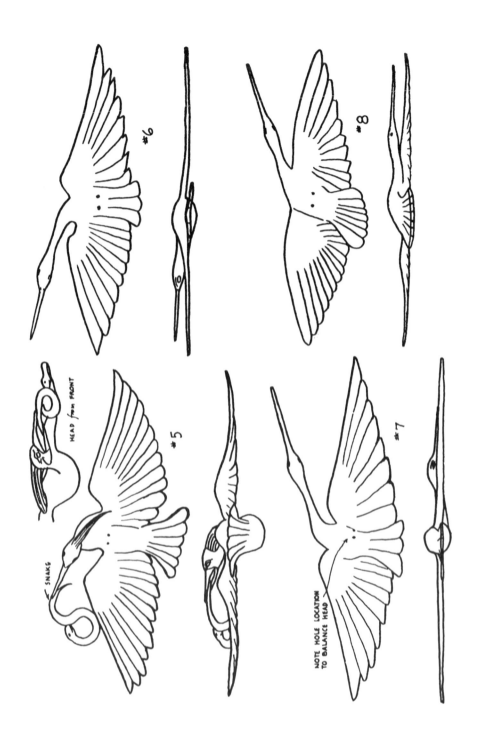

#6

#8

HEAD from FRONT

#5

SNAKE

#7

NOTE HOLE LOCATION
TO BALANCE HEAD

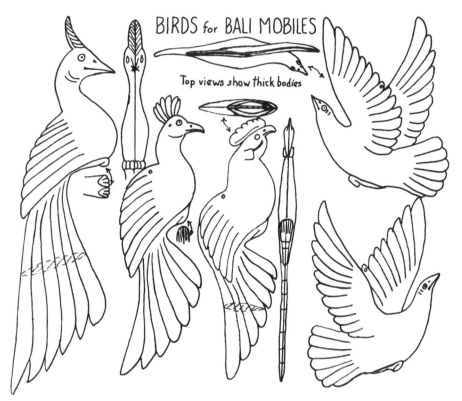

BIRDS for BALI MOBILES

Top views show thick bodies

Fig. 192. Side-profile birds are really double-sided low-relief carvings rounded at edges. Note detailing of claws, topknot and facial elements, but not of wing or tail. Bills are thickened for strength. Finish is gloss.

are carved. Both designs and carving are stylized; the birds are not quite realistic and the V-tool lines suggesting feathers are uniformly spaced. Also, the same design is done in both a light wood and ebony, so mobiles can be one color or two.

In my sketches, I have indicated approximate balance points, but exact ones will vary with relative wing thickness and other factors. You can determine precise balance by sticking a pin on a string into the bird's back or, for more exact location of center of gravity, by using two pins and attaining balance between them.

Designs can be cut out with a scroll saw. I used maple and mahogany rather than ebony, but any fairly hard wood would work quite well; it should be dense enough to resist breakage in thinner elements. Grain must

Fig. 193 (left). Three birds in light wood. Fig. 194 (right). Two in ebony.

go with the line of the wings in the case of top-profile birds, and vertically in the case of side-profile ones. I made lines and eyes of the design with a small and very sharp V-tool. Birds may be sanded if desired—the Balinese ones are—and finished with natural shoe polish.

In making the mobile, I used #18 piano wire (0.041-in [.010-cm] diameter) for the whiffletrees or spreaders, and a section of coat hanger for the top one. This is for full-size birds about 7 in (17.8 cm) long. The mobile was built up progressively, starting with lighter birds at the bottom, and thread lengths are 2 to 6 in (5.1 to 15.2 cm), the threads being monofilament nylon.

On the topside mobile pictured, there are four birds suspended from each end of an 18-in (45.6-cm) top whiffletree. Each arm has two light birds on a 4½-in (11.4-cm) whiffletree, balanced by one bird on a 6-in (15.2-cm) whiffletree; these three are balanced by the heaviest bird on an 8-in (20.3-cm) whiffletree.

Some adjusting of thread length must be done after assembly to assure proper clearance, of course, and all nylon knots must be secured with plastic cement or they will come undone. My mobile took up 30 in (76.2 cm) of space top to bottom, but this can be reduced by widening the support whiffletrees so birds can be hung closer together on shorter threads without interference.

CHAPTER XII

Knife-carved Birds in Relief

If the silhouette is cut out, it can be modelled with the knife alone

RELIEF CARVING ALMOST AUTOMATICALLY BRINGS to mind an array of chisels, but some relief carving doesn't demand them. The silhouette of a bird often identifies it, whether in-the-round or in relief, and with the clearance provided by the silhouette it is often possible to carve and model the figure with the knife alone—unless some deep concavity is involved—particularly if it has a rounded bottom. This assumes, of course, that the carver can keep a knife sharp and can cut the two sides of a V-groove parallel. It even assumes that he can, on occasion, imitate the cut of a gouge with a series of smaller knife cuts. When the figure is small and detailed, the knife is almost an essential anyway.

A bird's shape flows; it has no sharp angles. It should suggest flight, and properly carved it will do that, whether or not it is painted or mounted. I have recently realized that I have almost none of the bird carvings I have

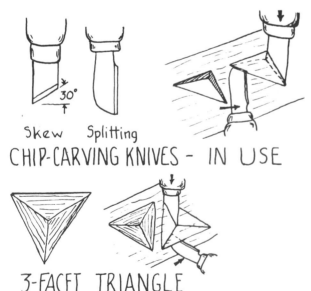

Skew   Splitting

CHIP-CARVING KNIVES – IN USE

3-FACET TRIANGLE

Fig. 195. Chip carving, an old German art brought here by the Pennsylvania Dutch, can be done with a pocketknife or special knives like those at left. Basic chip-carving patterns are triangles, diamonds or squares in all-over designs, or occasional spirals (see base of Fig. 198). The eagle, which is also chip-carved, as shown at right, was done with the knife alone, as were the designs above it.

Figs. 196–197. Fighting cocks, from a wall box.

Background fluted or stamped

Figs. 198–199. A chip-carved pipe rack. The eagle is 9 in (22.8 cm) tall, but only about ⅛ in (3.2 mm) deep.

81

Figs. 200–201 (left & below). These highly stylized birds were carved in Java in teak ¼ in (6.4 mm) thick. The largest is 6 in (15.2 cm) long. Fig. 202 (below left). Simple chick makes a neckerchief slide by Mack Sutter.

BIRD PANEL
Java-Teak
Pierced relief

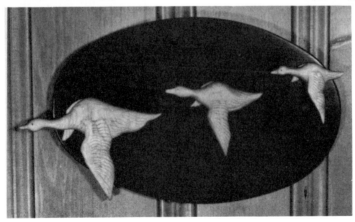

Fig. 203. One bird silhouette repeated in three sizes makes this panel on walnut. The birds I whittle from ¾-in (19.1-mm) white pine, showing only wing feathering, and no tinting.

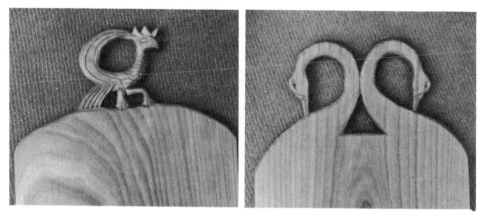

Figs. 204–205 (above). Broodplanken *is the Dutch word for these individual breadboards from Arnhem; mine are in cherry ½ × 8 × 11 in (1.3 × 20.3 × 27.9 cm), made with coping saw and pocketknife. Fig. 206 (below). A Dutch spoon rack, typical of many designs incorporating birds and flowers, and usually painted. Black areas are cut through.*

SPOON RACK

Black areas pierced

Gouge crescent

csc

csc

Slotted bar

This area is painted-floral designs

Polychrome & gilt

Ars Longa
Hindeloopen

Fig. 207 (left). Incised and tinted gourds from El Salvador, the larger about 6 in (15.2 cm). The smaller has a diaper pattern of wings, the larger birds and flowers. Both are created by shallow incising through the dark outer surface to expose lighter inner color.

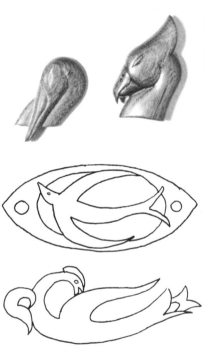

Figs. 208–209 (above). Barrettes and brooches depicting whole birds or just heads can be whittled in hard woods. Here are two walnut pins, a goose and a hawk, and two barrette patterns which can be carved in curving-grain wood around a knot.

Fig. 210. Earl Reichelsderfer, East Peoria, Illinois, carved these miniature silhouettes. He disregarded scale, which avoids making small birds like wrens almost microscopic when adjacent to big ones like eagles. Backs are flat, for wall mounting.

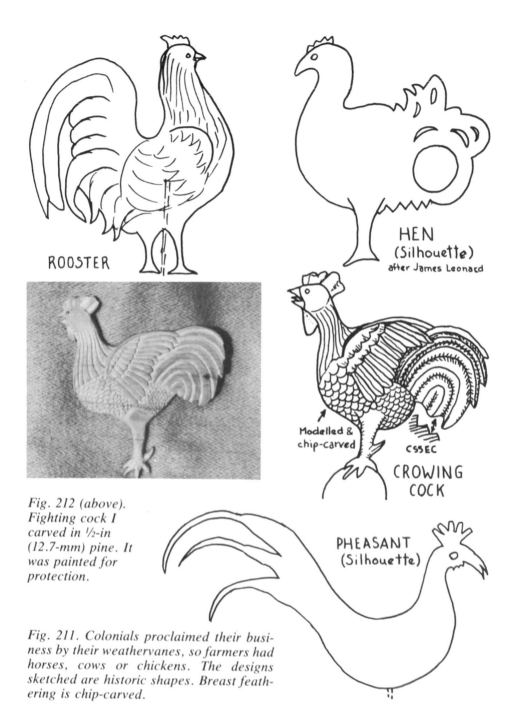

ROOSTER

HEN
(Silhouette)
after James Leonard

CROWING
COCK

Modelled &
chip-carved

CSSEC

PHEASANT
(Silhouette)

Fig. 212 (above). Fighting cock I carved in ½-in (12.7-mm) pine. It was painted for protection.

Fig. 211. Colonials proclaimed their business by their weathervanes, so farmers had horses, cows or chickens. The designs sketched are historic shapes. Breast feathering is chip-carved.

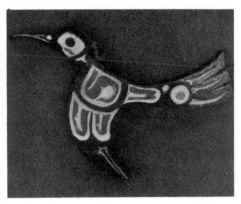

Fig. 213 (top left). Toraja-motif flying bird from Sulawesi, with inserted wings. Parts are shaped, then dipped in black matte paint. Decorative incising reveals white wood, which is tinted (Fig. 217). Fig. 214 (above). Haida hummingbird 8½ in (21.6 cm), tinted with oils. Fig. 215 (left). A 7-in (17.8-cm) swallow in ebony (see Fig. 222).

made; they go, one way or another, almost as fast as I carve them. This is not unusual; many carvers make a good living, or at least a good side income, from carving birds. Part of the answer is that even low-relief birds live a three-dimensional life; they can be free of the earth at will, while man cannot.

In this chapter and the next two, I have tried to show the variety possible in carving birds in relief—and for relief. In contrast to the carving of birds in-the-round, birds in relief are often stylized and usually simplified; there is little effort to depict every feather—even though feathers and legs are much easier. The primary purpose is to create something decorative. Also, a much smaller proportion of the birds carved in relief are painted or colored; the usual bird in relief is destined to be decorative.

Whittled birds in silhouette can be mounted on a background of wood or other material, or simply hung on a wall. If they are carved double-sided, they can be mounted in single or multiple mobiles (see the Balinese examples in Chapter XI). Also, rather than in pine or basswood, they can be carved in decorative woods.

Probably the simplest kind of relief carving is incising, in effect drawing

HUMMINGBIRD - Haida
After Dorothy Simpson

Colors
White-Hollowed & white
Black - Black
▨ - Red ▧ - Turquoise

Fig. 216 (above). Haida Indian hummingbird is pine, relief-carved. Fig. 217 (below). Toraja flying bird of Fig. 213 is an assembly.

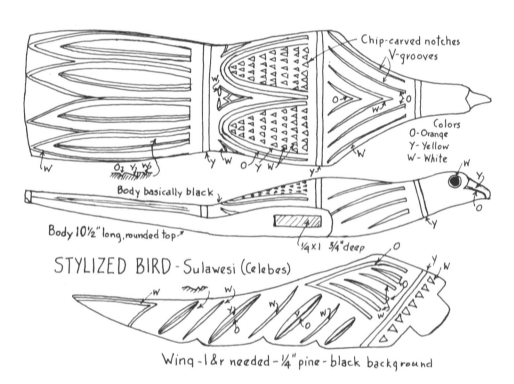

Chip-carved notches
V-grooves

Colors
O - Orange
Y - Yellow
W - White

Body basically black

Body 10½" long, rounded top

¼ × 1 ¾" deep

STYLIZED BIRD - Sulawesi (Celebes)

Wing - l & r needed - ¼" pine - black background

Fig. 218 (above). Jaegers in 10-in (25.4-cm) white pine are tinted with oils.

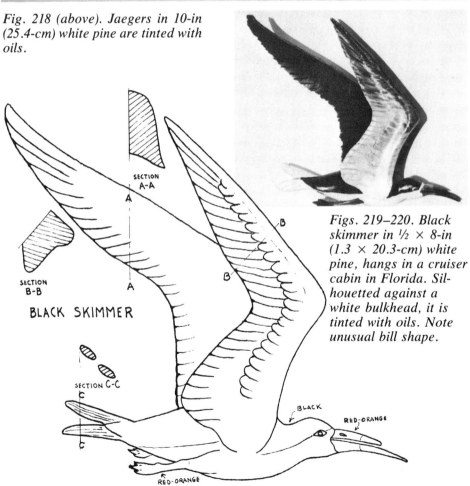

SECTION A-A

SECTION B-B

BLACK SKIMMER

SECTION C-C

A

A

B

B

C

C

BLACK

RED-ORANGE

RED-ORANGE

Figs. 219–220. Black skimmer in ½ × 8-in (1.3 × 20.3-cm) white pine, hangs in a cruiser cabin in Florida. Silhouetted against a white bulkhead, it is tinted with oils. Note unusual bill shape.

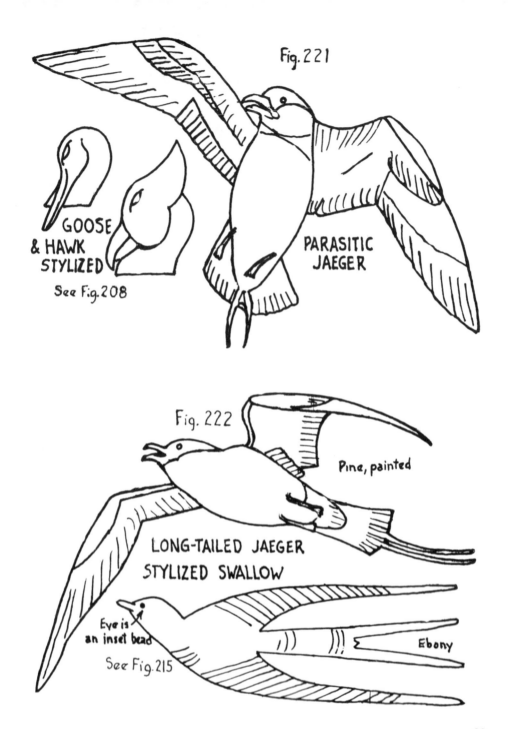

Fig. 221

GOOSE
& HAWK
STYLIZED

See Fig. 208

PARASITIC
JAEGER

Fig. 222

Pine, painted

LONG-TAILED JAEGER
STYLIZED SWALLOW

Eye is
an inset bead

See Fig. 215

Ebony

·Figs. 223–224.
These four
holly figures
are each about
1½ in (3.8 cm)
tall with base.
Note color
added on sway.

a picture by means of a tool, either a knife or a V-tool. In many countries, this work is done on gourds or other natural surfaces. It is essentially the same thing as scrimshanding, and may be finished similarly by filling the incised lines with a color. Also quite simple is chip carving, in which a pattern is created of triangles or other shapes made by cutting out chips or notches of suitable shape. I have shown examples of both of these, including a sketch of the basic cuts in chip carving.

While relief carving with the knife, make certain that the silhouette suggests the bird or the design. If this is true, the modelling is largely a matter of rounding up edges and inserting cuts to suggest eyes, bill and perhaps basic feathering. I have included here a number of patterns for silhouettes which can be sawed out of thin wood. From such essentially flat silhouettes, it is not too great a step to, birds such as those on cuckoo clocks, or such birds as the black skimmer or the jaeger, which are really only silhouettes copied from bird books and made three-dimensional.

On such pieces, much of the problem is the painting. I use oil pigments in varnish, but have seen birds done with enamels, acrylics or even a variety of stains. This assumes, of course, that the bird is carved in soft wood. I have made many pins and brooches with bird designs, but in hard woods, so finishing was merely polishing.

CHAPTER XIII

Chisel-carved Birds in Relief

Chisels speed the work and make special-shape cuts

WHEN A BIRD IS CARVED in relief against a background, or when it is to be carved quite large, chisels will speed and simplify the work, regardless of the wood. If the wood is hard, like cherry, walnut or even mahogany, chisels make it possible to produce more accurate shapes quickly and easily. It is not that difficult to learn to use them, and perhaps a short lesson is in order.

You will be concerned essentially with chisels in three general shapes. The simplest is the firmer. It is really a flat chisel sharpened from both sides so it can be used with either hand, and it has little tendency to dig in or run out. Firmers come in various widths from as small as ¹⁄₁₆ in (2 mm) to a couple of inches wide. You'll be concerned, most likely, only with the narrower ones up to ½ in (12.7 mm) wide.

Gouges are chisels with a curved edge, the degree of curvature being

Fig. 225. My front door is of teak, with three octagonal panels. I filled them with simple incised carvings of an owl, a squirrel and a rabbit. This is the owl, a caricature done almost entirely with a firmer, after some V-tool outlining. It has withstood the weather for almost 50 years, with occasional refinishing. The cracked panel is unusual for teak, and was probably caused by faulty door assembly.

Heavy & straight cuts
Heel of back hand pushes handle end
Near hand guides, prevents overcuts & slips

Light & curving cuts
Back hand presses forward & steers
Near hand restrains, rests on work

Side cuts & V-tool cuts
Back hand presses
Near hand pulls, rests on work

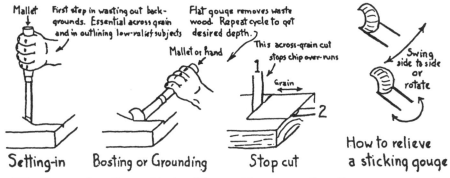

Mallet

First step in wasting out backgrounds. Essential across grain and in outlining low-relief subjects

Flat gouge removes waste wood. Repeat cycle to get desired depth.

Mallet or hand

This across-grain cut stops chip over-runs

Grain

Swing side to side or rotate

Setting-in **Bosting or Grounding** **Stop cut** **How to relieve a sticking gouge**

Fig. 226. *How to handle a chisel, with or without a mallet. Because a chisel's cutting edge is across the end instead of on one side, it must be pushed or driven into the work; thus carving with it is often a two-handed process (Fig. 11).*

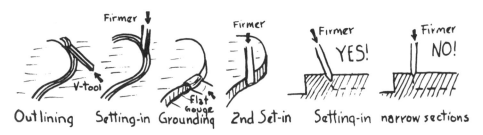

Firmer

Firmer

Firmer
YES!

Firmer
NO!

Outlining **Setting-in** **Grounding** **2nd Set-in** **Setting-in** **narrow sections**

V-tool

Flat Gouge

Fig. 227. *Proper setting-in and grounding are the keys to successful relief carving. These sketches may help you understand the principles of getting rid of background wood, always a chore. Further information, including chisel selection, is in Chapter I.*

called the sweep. The old English method was to number the gouge by the amount of sweep, a #3 gouge being almost flat, and a #9 or #10 being half round. Some toolmakers now are numbering the gouges to indicate the diameter of the circle of which the chisel is an arc; thus a #1 is a ¹⁄₁₆-in (2-mm) diameter sweep, and a #8 is a ⁸⁄₁₆- or ½-in (12.7-mm) diameter sweep. In addition, there are two specialized gouge shapes, the veiner—really a name for the ¹⁄₁₆-in (2-mm) half-round gouge used for putting veins in leaves, hair on heads and the like—and the fluter, with an arced bottom and high parallel sides, so in cross section it is U-shaped. The high sides permit it to carve a half-round flute without catching at the edges. A third shape, and my favorite, is the V-tool, like two flat chisels joined at an angle, so it cuts a vee in the wood. It is difficult to sharpen, but extremely useful.

Many bird carvers use the knife for small birds and the rasp for larger ones, but put in detail with gouges and V-tools, sometimes homemade. In carving something like a stylized pattern of breast feathers, it is very helpful to have a gouge with the correct diameter of circle outline, particularly a half-round one.

Chisels, of course, differ from the knife in that the cutting edge is crosswise of the blade, so cutting is achieved mainly by pushing. This is an arm motion rather than a hand motion. The commonest whittling cut is simply closing the hand, which gives very close control, while the arm motion required by a chisel does not. Thus, professional carvers use a longer chisel and hold it with both hands; one hand pushes the chisel and the other guides it, and actually keeps it from cutting too far because the wood varies in hardness or because for some other reason the cutting speed has changed. In recent years, it has become common for whittlers turned carvers to use short-handled chisels, either with a palm knob like an engraver's burin or with a round handle. These really are more suited to one-handed use, but must be handled very carefully to prevent cutting the other hand, particularly if the latter is being used as a vise. This is common in bird carving, particularly for in-the-round work and in relief carving of silhouettes, as discussed in Chapter XII. A panel of any size can be laid on a bench and pushed against a stop (see Chapter I), thus reducing the danger.

In panel or similar relief carving, the primary operation is to get unwanted background out of the way. This is usually done by a process called grounding. After the outline desired has been drawn on the wood, the first step in grounding is setting-in, done with narrow firmers and

CARDINALS - plaque or box top

Figs. 228–229 (far left and center). This pair of cardinals is in rosewood, 3 × 5 in (7.6 × 12.7 cm), with texture replacing the normal colors. Note how feather lines on wings darken them, compared with the smooth body and background. It might have been better to hatch, stamp or roughen the background as well, to make it recede. Flat surfaces reflect light, hence appear lighter in color. Fig. 230 (far right). This panel from 9th-century Parambanan Temple in Jogjakarta, Java, is one of at least a dozen featuring birds. They are about 3 ft (91.4 cm) tall.

gouges, and preferably with a light mallet to drive them. The tool is driven vertically into the wood just outside the sketched outline to sever the fibres. The next operation is to remove the background wood up to the set-in line with a flat gouge.

There are obviously several precautions to be taken. It may be easier for you to start in soft wood, and outline the subject with a V-tool before you set-in (see Figs. 226 and 227). Next, never set in more than ⅛ in (3.2 mm) at a time, even though you may have thin tools, because you will crush the fibres at the sides of the cut and make trouble for yourself later.

Thirdly, when you are setting-in around narrow sections, particularly across grain, be *very* careful—drive the outlining chisel in at an angle *away* from the thin section (see Figs. 226 and 227) to prevent breakouts in that section. A general rule for this is to slope the chisel when the section is ¼ in (6.4 mm) wide or less in soft woods, and reducing to ⅛ in (3.2 mm) or so in hard wood, unless they tend to split, as mahogany does. When the

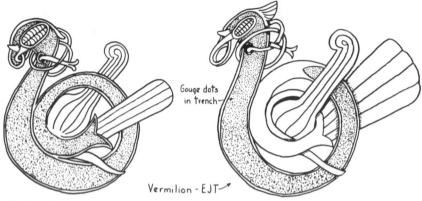

Gouge dots
in trench

Vermilion - EJT

CELTIC BIRD BROOCH ···& modification··· CELTIC CARDINAL

Fig. 232. This screech owl I carved on a walnut napkin ring for a collector. It is 2 in (5.1 cm) square, on a circlet with a 1½-in (3.8-cm) belled bore.

Figs. 231 (top) & 233 (above right). A Celtic brooch, with its interlacing elements, intrigues me into a modification with crest and more prominent tail (see top). My version is in ½-in (12.7-mm) vermilion, mounted on an African-wood-veneered panel about 7 in (17.8 cm) square. Sketches in Fig. 231 compare the two. Note the effect of stamping the background and some areas so they recede.

Surface rough
Feather outlines

Veiner cuts

⅛" gouge marks

TSIMSHIAN SHAMAN'S SOUL CATCHER (B.C.)
A bird (either double-headed or two sides of one head) interpreted by Willard L. Jones. Area between heads is backbone, ribs & claws.

ROOSTING QUETZAL
Guatemala - Mahogany

Fig. 234 (above). This is how a Northwest Coast Indian saw a bird with supernatural powers. It is a low-relief carving, painted, and typical of many interpretations there. They required some training to understand at all.

Figs. 235–237. The quetzal is Guatemala's national bird. Here the carver has suggested its brilliant colors with texture, because his wood is mahogany. These carvings are quite large, 12 in (30.5 cm) for the roosting bird, 2½ and 3 ft (76.2 and 91.4 cm) for the flying ones— carved in facing pairs! Wood is 1 in (2.5 cm) thick, more than half cut away on tails and wing edges.

Veiner or V-tool cuts →

← CSSC.

← Original 3' long

Original 2½' long

Note: Both designs are made in facing pairs

FLYING QUETZALS (Guatemalan national bird) – Mahogany

Fig. 238 (above). Stylized birds in a 19th-century Irish panel at the Metropolitan Museum of Art.

Fig. 239 (top right). The dining room of an inn at Lake Pahoe, Chile, had about 100 chairs with carved backs of local scenes. One Indian carved them all. This one features emperor penguins.

Fig. 240 (right). Ted Haag of Tualatin, Oregon, carved this pose of a flying duck against a scalloped background. Only pinion feathers are shown.

Fig. 241. Sign for the Quail Hill Inn, Old Somerville, New Jersey, is unusual in that the quail is not appliquéd but trench-carved. Trench carving was the earliest form of Egyptian relief carving.

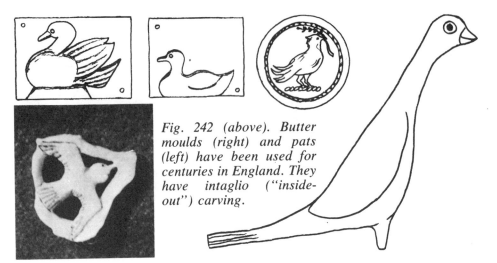

Fig. 242 (above). Butter moulds (right) and pats (left) have been used for centuries in England. They have intaglio ("inside-out") carving.

Fig. 243 (above). Bird designs can be adapted to many shapes. This cross section of a walrus tusk became a pendant with scrimshanded bird.

Fig. 244 (above). Very audacious was this Mexican stylization, a double-sided stand-up bird, painted white with closely spaced black spots.

outside wood has been "wasted away"—cut out—the set-in line can be shaved to vertical.

Lastly, if you plan grounding deeper than ⅛ in (3.2 mm)—and most of the time it will be deeper than that—be very careful as you set-in the deeper steps; make sure you follow the original line down. Also, do not set-in any deeper than you intend to carve the background, because the cut line the chisel makes will disfigure your final carving.

The background can be perfectly flat, of course, but it is customary to leave it a bit rough, either with gouge marks or with a stippled effect or other pattern arrived at by driving in a stamp. Such texturing serves to break up the light hitting the plaque, making the background appear darker and deeper than it actually is. If the background is left smooth, any texturing done on the bird itself will make it appear darker than the ground, which is undesirable.

It is also possible to accentuate the distinction between subject and background by staining the ground a bit darker. I combine this with what I call "antiquing," namely, sealing the surface of the finished carving with a flat varnish, then applying a darker stain and wiping it off immediately from the surface, leaving some stain in the cut lines to make them darker. *You must seal the wood first.*

The adze was the major carving tool of the Egyptians and is still used by Italians, South Pacific islanders, Africans, and our Northwest Coast Indians, who developed their own forms long ago. Adzes are uncommon in northern Europe and the United States for carving.

Fig. 247 (below). Owl incorporated in a pillar design.

Figs. 245, 246 & 248. D-adze made of an old half-round file with maple handle in bird form by Hugh C. Minton, Jr. (see Fig. 13). Fig. 245 (far left) shows the handle base. Fig. 248 (below) Forms of adze developed by Northwest Coast Indians.

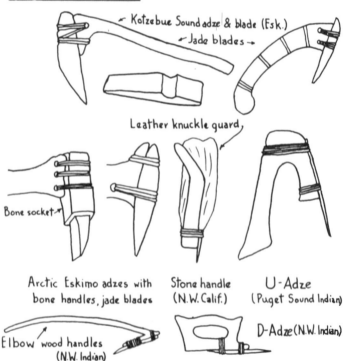

Kotzebue Sound adze & blade (Esk.)

Jade blades →

Leather knuckle guard

Bone socket

Arctic Eskimo adzes with bone handles, jade blades

Stone handle (N.W. Calif.)

U-Adze (Puget Sound Indian)

Elbow wood handles (N.W. Indian)

D-Adze (N.W. Indian)

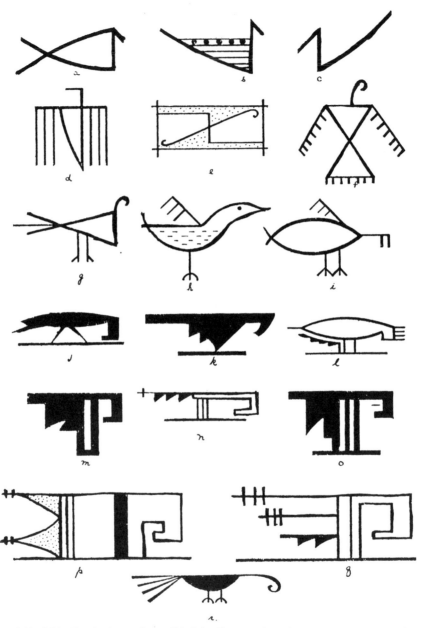

Figs. 249–250. Evolution of the Bird in Decorative Art *was written in 1916 by Kenneth M. Chapman. These two pages show symbolic variations in the design of a bird, and are American Indian in origin. They can be incised, inlaid or relief-carved.*

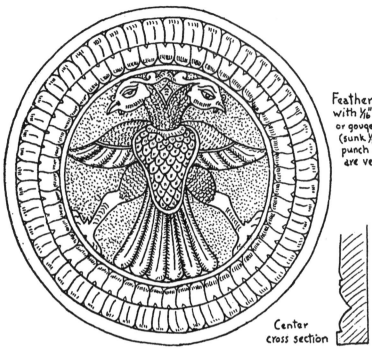

Feather pattern is made with 1/16" semi-circle stamp or gouge. Background (sunk 1/8") is stippled with punch or veiner. Details are veiner or V-tool lines.

Center cross section

Figs. 251–252. These two panels from Sri Lanka (Ceylon) depict the Hansa, or sacred goose. The circular sketch has a lotus-petal border, while the other is a 14-in (35.6-cm) diameter panel with three geese interlocked. Note how the necks of the birds are elongated and interlaced, with the wings of each bird crowded towards its tail. The wood is a light color like maple.

Fig. 253. A shower curtain in a Mexican hotel provided this design. It conventionalized birds and deer to fit an area, filling each body center with a pattern that suggests a center of life.

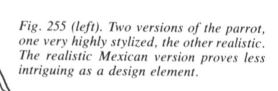

PARROTS
Mexico →
← New Guinea

Fig. 254 (above). German carvers make cuckoo-clock fronts on a production basis, working on five frames at once, held by pins side-by-side on a bench. Only chisels are used, and frames are designed so that a series of gouges make progressive cuts. I picked up this frame in Germany in 1973 without the pattern, so had to guess at the design when I carved it.

Fig. 255 (left). Two versions of the parrot, one very highly stylized, the other realistic. The realistic Mexican version proves less intriguing as a design element.

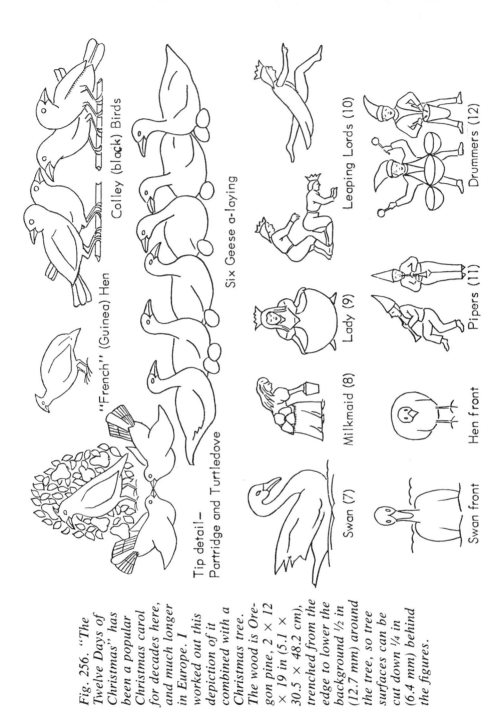

Colley (black) Birds

"French" (Guinea) Hen

Six Geese a-laying

Tip detail—
Partridge and Turtledove

Leaping Lords (10)

Drummers (12)

Lady (9)

Pipers (11)

Milkmaid (8)

Hen front

Swan (7)

Swan front

Fig. 256. "The Twelve Days of Christmas" has been a popular Carol for decades here, and much longer in Europe. I worked out this depiction of it combined with a Christmas tree. The wood is Oregon pine, 2 × 12 × 19 in (5.1 × 30.5 × 48.2 cm), trenched from the edge to lower the background ½ in (12.7 mm) around the tree, so tree surfaces can be cut down ¼ in (6.4 mm) behind the figures.

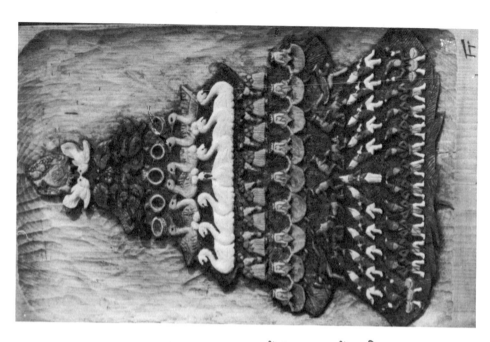

Fig. 257. First, the partridge is an English bird. We call the ruffed grouse a partridge in the Northeast, and the bobwhite quail a partridge in the South. "Turtledoves" are not grey like ours, but white. "French hens" is a puzzler, but I finally came up with the idea that it means guinea hens. The four "colored" or "canary" birds that we tend to sing about is incorrect; the word really is "colley," meaning black. Add in costumes for lords and ladies that suit an earlier era, and uniforms and instruments for pipers and drummers that do as well . . . the sketches tell the story. On a panel like this, lay out the tree first, then position the designs in proper number, line by line. I trenched the background with a ½-in (12.7-mm) flat gouge and left it rough. Figures require much detailing—I used a knife—and are helped by color. The tree surface can be lined with V-tool or veiner to suggest needles, then tinted a dark green. The background can be "antiqued" with light tan. Before any coloring, seal the area with flat varnish, or cross-grain portions will soak up too much color.

CHAPTER XIV

Escher's Birds Can Be 3D

Woodcuts and sketches converted into panel carvings

M. C. ESCHER, DUTCH ARTIST, mathematician and draftsman who died in 1972, has been a favorite of America's younger set for more than a decade. His works are largely intricate patterns which involve interlocking or repetitive units, distortion or perspective peculiarities that result in such impossible things as water running uphill. I first became a devotee when I saw his "Sky and Water—1," probably his best-known work.

In "Sky and Water—1," made in 1938 and about 17½ in (44 cm) square, a repeated flying goose becomes less distinct as a fish emerges between geese. I suddenly realized that the woodcut could be converted into a relief panel if the elements above the middle were in relief, fading to nothing, and the elements below were in *intaglio*, or reverse relief, in which the carving is inside out, so it is actually a mould below the surface. The idea would work well because the geese would be standing out in "air," while the fish would be beneath the surface of the "water." Also, the design was well suited for a fireboard for which I had a commission; the people concerned like both birds and fish, and the fireplace front to be covered required a design clearly visible from above.

My size was 31 × 34 in (78.8 × 86.4 cm), roughly double that of the original, so it would require a bit of addition at the sides, and more detail would have to be put in the top goose and bottom fish (the latter was just cross-hatched in the original). Also, I decided that I could tilt the 1-in (2.5-cm) teak panel back about 15 degrees, for easier viewing.

Intaglio carving is difficult because it forces the carver to think "inside

Fig. 258. An old 1 × 6 × 20-in (2.5 × 15.2 × 50.8-cm) white-pine shelf (with burns) was my first test of intaglio carving for the Escher piece.

out," and because there are so many precise concavities that bent gouges and other tools are almost a must. I tried carving bird and fish in intaglio in a 1 × 6 × 20-in (2.5 × 15.2 × 50.8-cm) pine board; this reinforced my opinion that it should be the fish in intaglio. Layout was largely a matter of enlarging by the method of squares and adding on at the sides; I used a border similar to Escher's, of ragged parallel horizontal lines.

I arbitrarily selected ⅜ in (9.5 mm) as the maximum carving depth at top and bottom; this gave plenty of depth for modelling the elements, and

Fig. 259. A 1 × 30 × 34-in (2.5 × 76.2 × 86.3-cm) fireboard (screen for an unused fireplace) is supported by two 2 × 3 × 5-in (5.1 × 7.6 × 12.7-cm) walnut blocks and rear aluminum legs inside the fireplace so it is tilted 15° for easy viewing. It is a 3D copy of Escher's famous "Sky and Water—I."

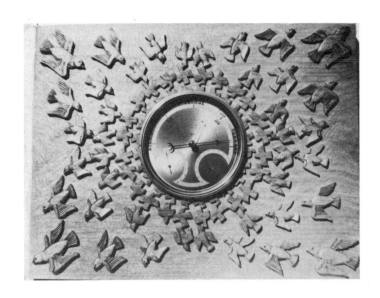

Figs. 260–261.
Flying-bird panel
of 2 × 14 × 17-
in (5.1 × 35.6 ×
43.2-cm) blond
limba is thick
enough for the
barometer body.
Escher's design
that framed a
clock was
slightly wider in
proportion and
had an added
ring or two of
crosses at the
center. Back-
ground is
rounded at the
edges and
roughened.

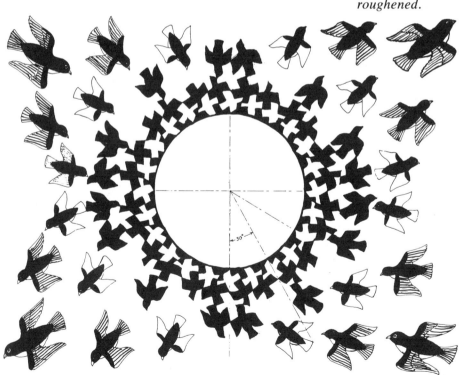

DESIGN "SIMPLIFICATION"

Fig. 262. My version, in ¼-in (6.4-mm) maple and mahogany.

ORIGINAL ESCHER DESIGN   "SIMPLIFIED" VERSION (EJT)

Fig. 263. Escher's sketch projected a wingtip and got a good design; I "simplified" mine and got a faulty one. I lost point contact and color balance.

allowed me to slope the background to ⅛ in (3.2 mm) at the middle. I finished with a coat of varnish, then waxed for ease in cleaning and set the panel on walnut blocks.

This panel was so successful and intriguing that it led me into half a dozen other Escher copies, including one that worked out well and one that did not—both involving birds. I first saw a group of birds that Escher had sketched on a postcard sent to a friend. I left the postal and tried to remember the sketch when I got home. I "simplified" it unwittingly—and got it slightly wrong. My initial Escher copy was birds of maple and mahogany, scrollsawed to two interlocking shapes with wings spread out; the birds fit together as they would in a jigsaw puzzle. Mine fitted all right, but there was a poor joining of one bird's wing and another's head that Escher would not have permitted. On my next opportunity, I sketched the birds correctly; try them and see how well they look.

Another design, executed in primavera, involved two flights of birds diagonally across the panel in opposite directions, the birds evolving into crosses in a center swirl. Escher used it to frame a clock; I used it to frame a barometer, which is perhaps a little too "busy" and dominant for the design. This piece is monolithic, and the individual birds are stained slightly to amplify the effect of modelling and to make them stand out, with the background lighter—the reverse of usual practice. After ten years or so, I found it necessary to restain the birds; sunlight had faded the color in the Vermont house where it hangs.

CHAPTER XV

Polyglot Panels Group Birds

Low-relief silhouettes and texturing make species identifiable

IN THE LATE SIXTIES, I carved the "bug tree," a 12-ft (4-m) dead apple surfaced with giant, low-relief depictions of familiar "bugs." This led to a commission for a "bug door" and production of eight teak panels depicting realistic birds, insects, animals, flowers, fish, saurians, and so on (see Fig. 267).

This commission has in turn led to perhaps a score of others, including:

Fig. 264 (left). One of four Rackham panels in walnut. This one depicts 28 Aesop fables, including roosters, crane, crow, owl, etc., in the montage. Fig. 265 (right). Layout is largely by "feel" and just precedes carving. I also alternate grounding and modelling for variety. Grounding is only ⅜ in (9.5 mm) deep at most, and small gouges and a V-tool do much of the work.

Fig. 266 (right). This all-bird panel in teak is ¾ × 9⅜ × 18 in (1.9 × 23.8 × 45.7 cm) and contains more than 50 birds. Poses and species were selected for ease of identifica-tion. Local "birders" have identified most by sight. It is one of six panels on a door in Ghent, New York.

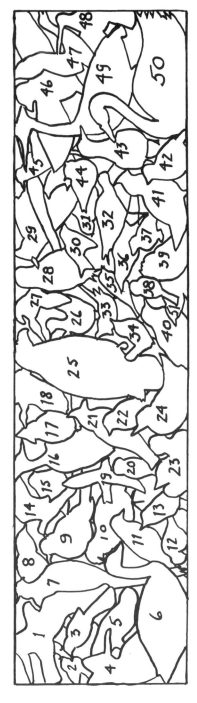

Fig. 267 (top). This bird panel, my first, is in teak 1 × 9 × 30¾ in (2.5 × 22.9 × 78.1 cm). It has 51 birds in low relief, hopefully in recognizable poses. Fig. 268 (above). This diagram was primarily for the client's use in identification of species, and was accompanied by the key list on the next page, made after the carving; the design was on the wood itself.

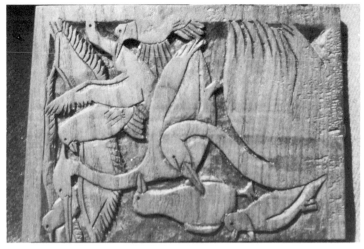

Fig. 269. To show what I planned for this door, I made this sample in a teak scrap. Door carvings were not protected against weather except with teak oil periodically (except for Mazola® recently), although entirely exposed.

AMERICAN BIRDS—Identification

Note: Bird guides are good sources for silhouettes, but must be alternated to avoid monotony. Dark areas can be suggested by texturing; avoid it on lighter areas like breasts. To get a very dark area, suggesting black or other deep color, try cross-hatching. This can be "antiqued" (darkened by staining) in finishing. Darkening the background will make the carving appear deeper and make the bird silhouettes stand out. I use walnut stain to antique teak, and dark walnut to antique walnut. Do not use black.

1. Duck hawk
2. Golden-crowned kinglet
3. Catbird
4. Kingfisher
5. Pigeon hawk
6. Canada goose
7. Ring-necked pheasant
8. Brown thrasher
9. Hermit thrush
10. Black gyrfalcon
11. Dove
12. Goldfinch
13. Green heron
14. Arctic tern
15. Quail or bobwhite
16. Ivory-billed woodpecker
17. Cardinal
18. Yellow-crowned night heron
19. Chimney swift
20. Burrowing owl
21. Cedar waxwing
22. Bluebird
23. Hooded merganser
24. Gannet
25. Bald eagle
26. Greater snow goose
27. Canvasback duck
28. Duck hawk
29. Blue jay
30. Redstart
31. Crossbill
32. Solitary sandpiper
33. Tufted titmouse
34. Marsh wren
35. Painted bunting
36. Yellow-billed cuckoo
37. Puffin
38. Chickadee
39. Screech owl
40. Robin (Note #51 next)
41. Ruffed grouse
42. Kingbird
43. Booby
44. Horned lark
45. Frigate bird
46. Osprey
47. Mallard duck
48. Hummingbird
49. Great white heron
50. Swan
51. Swainson's warbler (next to #40)

A list like the one above is provided for each panel's key drawing.

a walrus tusk decorated with birds and flowers; a wooden shoe with flowers alone; and a variety of panels in various woods, most incorporating birds and flowers, but one a second door of six panels and one showing the avocational history of a friend—hidden by birds and flowers.

These panels are unusual in that there is no background and no real pattern in the sense that elements blend. They are more nearly akin to jigsaw puzzles in that the birds and/or blooms are set-in without respect to scale, but carefully selected to fit together physically. Thus, an eagle may be depicted as only three or four times the size of a wren, but the individual low-relief birds are identifiable, and indeed, the client is provided with a sketch and identification chart to accompany the panel.

These are not fanciful, but realistic, depictions in low relief. Thus, it is advisable not to associate two birds with crests or of similar body shape,

Fig. 270 (left). Panel in vermilion (amboina), 12 × 19 in (30.5 × 48.3 cm). Fig. 271 (below right). With wood from the top of an antique mahogany table, this panel contains 109 flowers, 6 birds, a butterfly, a moth, and a gnome. It is ¾ × 11¾ × 16 in (1.9 × 29.8 × 40.6 cm).

but rather to contrast them as widely as possible. Also, avoid depicting several birds with almost identical silhouettes and similar arrangement of coloring (the colors themselves do not matter; it is the *arrangement* of colors that is a factor in identification, and must be simulated by texture).

In the course of time, I have made a variety of panels in a variety of woods, including walnut, mahogany and vermilion. Some of the variations in content and material are shown here, including a "mixed" panel of birds and flowers. I do *not* lay out the entire panel before I start; instead, I begin at one corner and draw in elements just in advance of carving them. This works out better than a pencilled layout would, because spacing can be worked out better. It also avoids the necessity of checking back on lost source references, particularly when I am using four or five texts for a composite panel. I make the drawing *after* the panel is done—for identification only.

The most complex panels I have attempted thus far are a set of four based on the illustrations of Arthur Rackham, the famous English illustrator of fairy tales, who died in 1939, but whose popular books are in print again. I converted his pen sketches into low relief, in some cases selecting only a portion of an illustration because it suited my design. *Aesop's Fables*, *Grimms' Fairy Tales*, *Andersen's Fairy Tales* and a panel of other tale tellers like Perrault and Shakespeare make up the set. They are in walnut, two roughly 13 × 20 in (33.0 × 51.0 cm), and two roughly 9½ × 23 in (24.1 × 58.4 cm)—the maximum sizes of boards I had.

To apply these panels to a door, I have used screws topped by plugs rather than an adhesive. Thus, the panels can be removed at any time, and the plugs, trepanned from the same wood as the panels and matched for color and grain, hide the screws. Also, attaching in this way makes it possible to take up slight warpage and to allow differential expansion.

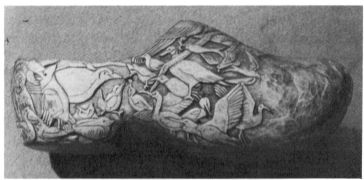

Fig. 272. This willow shoe fits me; its mate features fish. Together they won an art-show award.

CHAPTER XVI

An Aerie of Eagles

They are popular carving subjects worldwide

CURRENT POPULARITY OF THE DECOY DUCK in the Eastern United States has perhaps eclipsed the often-caricatured owl, traditional goose and other birds in terms of numbers carved, but the longtime leader—the eagle—still remains a strong favorite. The eagle is an important symbol in American history. It is featured in the seal of the United States. (John Adams and Thomas Jefferson put it there in 1782; Ben Franklin preferred a turkey.) In such remote areas as the South Pacific, the sea eagle is the stuff of legend. So it seems only sensible to devote a special chapter to this mighty bird.

The eagle can be done in-the-round as a standing or hanging piece, but is probably easier depicted in relief carving, partly because of the difficulty and fragility of the feathering when detailed. In size, it can range from tiny earrings to heroic proportions, and is made in a variety of poses. It has been stylized so often and in so many different ways that there is a book published by Dover depicting them. It would be hopeless to attempt to

Fig. 273 (left). Poplar eagle on a maple ball, 15 in (38.1 cm) tall. Fig. 274 (right). Pine eagle 3 ft (91.4 cm) tall in a Maine museum. Both are traditional designs.

Fig. 275 (above). The largest eagle I've seen is at the Shelburne (Vermont) Museum. It has a wingspread of 20 ft (6.1 m), is carefully feathered and well-shaped.

Fig. 276 (above right). Mahogany eagle finished with white pigment on head and yellow on bill and legs, wiped down. It is 15 in (38.1 cm) tall.

Fig. 277 (right). Pine stooping eagle. Fig. 278 (below). Walrus-ivory earrings differ in design: one eagle flies, the other stoops. The eagle on the pendant is also stooping.

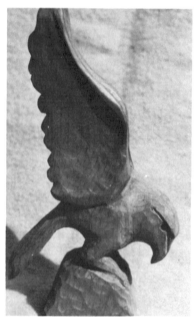

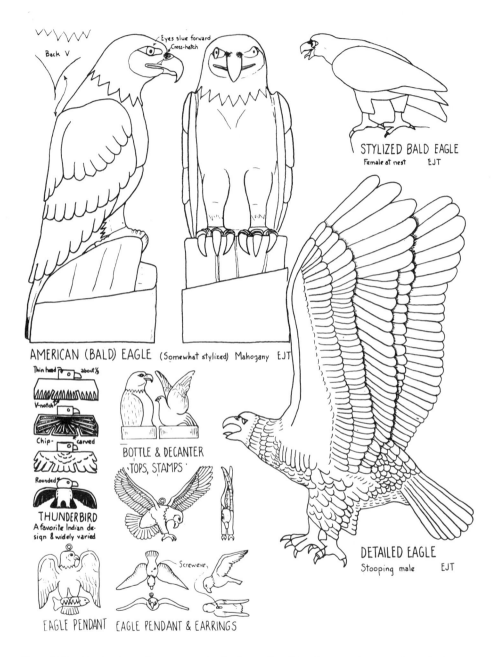

Fig. 279. Typical eagle poses, including the Northwest Coast Thunderbird at lower left, very stylized, and four designs I executed in walrus ivory.

Figs. 280–282. Three low-relief eagles. The eagle with scroll (top) is 2 in (5.1 cm) thick and more than 30 in (76.2 cm) long and was carved by Matilda Smith to grace an Indiana mantel. The pine eagle with broken chain (bottom) is by Michael DeNike and is 36 in (91.4 cm) wide. Beak and claws are gold-leafed, the chain silver-leafed. The eagle with arrow (center) tops a plaque.

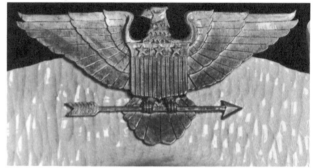

Figs. 283–285 (below). Three Mexican efforts at eagles, two by Indians showing the eagle, snake and cactus of the Mexican coat of arms; the other in horn as the handle of a machete.

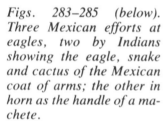

Figs. 286–287. Horn is shaped, sawed and scratch-carved into these Javanese spoons. One is an eagle, the other a dragon.

SPOON HANDLES
Java - Pierced cow horn

show all the variety, but I have made a selection here that includes a number of types, mostly from this country, but some from abroad.

Anatomical details are important in carving eagles. Such elements as the forward-placed eyes, the hooked bill, the neck ruff on the bald eagle, the claw arrangement, wing shape and feathering are very important, particularly if you are carving a flying pose. Many sculptors have not detailed the feathering at all, attaining their likeness by the silhouette, and maintaining that the observer doesn't see the detailed feathering anyway; people rarely get that close to eagles.

There may be something psychological about the preference for eagles—something in the nature of man that admires the raptor, because we tend to carve our eagles looking fierce, if not in an attacking stoop. One of the unexpected and relatively unnoticed uses of eagle designs is on the old German cuckoo clocks, which, after all, were associated usually with hunting scenes, with the eagle suggesting the hunter.

A motif similar to that on German cuckoo clocks appeared on American wooden-works clocks during the period from Andrew Jackson's presidency (1829–37), until brass works took over much later in the century—the so-called American Empire period. Initially, the splats (the top decorations on a clock) depicted an eagle, acanthus leaves, pineapples, paws or various birds and beasts. (These clocks sold for $8 complete, so you can imagine how much a carver got for the splat, how fast he had to work, and why he never signed his work.) Eagles were first used on stately clocks like the long-case types, particularly on eight-day wood-movement and 30-hour pendulum ones. Each maker had his own design, probably made by one or two carvers. The eagles all share a family resemblance, suggesting a common design ancestor. Carving conventions, such as those for feathers,

1. Chauncey Ives 30-hr long case. Rare

2. G&E Bartholomew 30-hr long pendulum

3. Riley Whiting #2 (Note differences)

4. Marsh-Gilbert 8-day.

5. Ely Terry & Son 8-day.   S.B. Terry

6. Rare

7. Silas Hoadley 30-hr. Note shield

8. Universal Eagle- many 30-hr clocks

9. Hopkins & Alfred   Rare

10. Putnam Bailey - One of a kind?

Fig. 288. American Empire eagle clock splats, from Sheldon Hock.

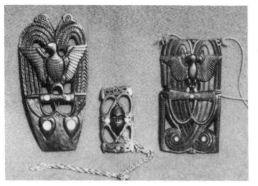

Figs. 289–291 (left). Ebony
pendants from the Tro-
briand Islands, Papua
New Guinea. The sea
eagle standing on a drum
is the national coat of
arms. Insets are paua
shell.

¼" thick

4¾"
5¾"

PENDANTS
Ebony. Pierced areas
in black; nacre inlays cross-hatched.

Fig. 292. Neck-
erchief slide by
Mack Sutter shows
the Boy Scout eagle
emblem.

Fig. 293. Bicenten-
nial bottle caps were
in mahogany. They
take ¾-in (19.1-mm)
corks.

122

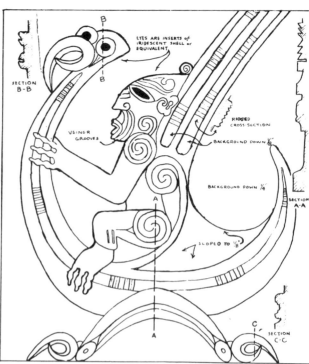

Figs. 294–295. Maori legend has it that the god Pourangahua on an eagle (Fig. 290) came from Hawaiki (the Milky Way) to settle New Zealand. My foot-square plaque is in dense black walnut with abalone-shell eyes.

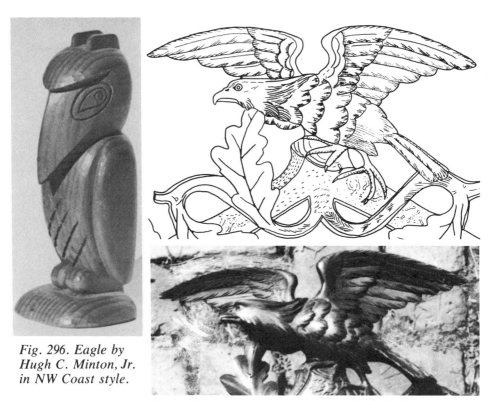

Fig. 296. Eagle by
Hugh C. Minton, Jr.
in NW Coast style.

Figs. 297–298 (right). The eagle appears on German cuckoo clocks as a splat
decoration. This one is from a clock bought by my parents in 1907 from Sears
Roebuck for $12.

are repeated. Some designs have crests, others do not, but very few designs have the eagle facing left. (I seem to recall that a left-facing eagle is considered cowardly and unpatriotic by purists.)

To show what all this was like, I have sketched a group based on research by Sheldon Hoch of White Plains, New York, who has carved copies of all the old splats, or photographs of them, that he could find. Note that both Terry designs, a famous name in wooden-works clocks, use a scroll (Fig. 288: 5 & 6), and that Silas Hoadley reinforced the patriotic motif with a shield (Fig. 288: 7). This design also had "the union be preserved" carved on the case. Only two birds have feet (Fig. 288: 9 & 10); they were carved by the same Connecticut man for a New York company. Competing makers eventually made many one-of-a-kind splats, depicting whatever the customer wanted, like the rooster (Fig. 288: 10).

CHAPTER XVII

Birds Make Pierced Panels

Japanese screens are bold treatments, including foliage

THE JAPANESE CARVE PIERCED screen panels to decorate, yet let air through shrines and temples; these often have bird or fish motifs. The panels shown here are examples. Three are from the Shitaya Shinto Shrine in Tokyo. They were carved in the thirties (although the shrine itself is 1,200 years old) in Japanese cypress by Mokoyurido Keiun. They are double-sided, because they are under the eaves over a sacred well, at which visitors purify themselves before they enter the shrine proper.

Pierced panels are also quite common in Indian and Chinese carving, but the Chinese tend to make geometric patterns (an entire book is devoted to Chinese carved lattices) and the Indians fill in spaces in their patterns with tracery or screening, probably to keep birds out. The Japanese patterns tend to be bigger, bolder and thicker, with colorful painting. The open spaces make for easier carving, but might permit breakage and warpage.

Of particular interest in these panels is the stylized water, always a difficult carving element. Also, the leaves are quite realistic although enlarged, and the birds tend to be stylized as well.

If such panels intrigue, be sure you use a straight-grained and clear piece of a wood not too likely to warp. Teak would be ideal, but expensive. Basswood or mahogany can be used, but must be protected against the atmosphere. Cedar or cypress might work well, or even clear white pine. In carving, it is advisable to leave some support between elements until heavy carving is completed, particularly if both faces are carved.

Fig. 299. Note the depth of carving and the bold treatment of this duck swimming at the Meiji Shrine, Tokyo. The water is exceptionally well-stylized.

Figs. 300–302 (above) & 303–305 (opposite page). Three of the four panels at the Shitaya Shrine, Tokyo. They are in cypress and mounted under the eaves, so the elaborate painting and openwork carving are not exposed to rain. They are in very deep relief, almost in-the-round. White areas are prayer papers stuck into openings.

Index